the art of *storytelling*

✳

EASY STEPS TO PRESENTING AN UNFORGETTABLE STORY

JOHN WALSH

Moody Publishers
Chicago

The Art of Storytelling

Copyright © 2003

by JOHN WALSH

Editorial services provided by Julie-Allyson Ieron for Joy Media.
Cover and Interior design by Paetzold Associates, St. Charles, Illinois.

A Teacher's Guide has been prepared for this book. For information,
go to www.christianstorytelling.com.

Library of Congress Cataloging-in-Publication Data

Walsh, John (John, D.), 1945–
   The art of storytelling : easy steps to presenting an unforgettable story /
John Walsh.
   p. cm.
ISBN: 0-8024-3306-5
1. Public Speaking. 2. Storytelling. 3. Anecdotes. I. Title
PN4193.I5 W35 2003
808.5'43—dc 21

                                                                    2002151128

ISBN: 0-8024-3306-5

1 3 5 7 9 10 8 6 4 2

Printed in the United States of America.

Table of Contents

*

FOURTEEN STEPS
TO PREPARING AN UNFORGETTABLE STORY

SEVEN TOOLS
FOR PRESENTING AN UNFORGETTABLE STORY

FOUR PLACES
TO GIVE AN UNFORGETTABLE STORY

APPENDICES

Prologue:

✳

A PERSONAL WORD

> *Speaking had been next to impossible for me, exposing myself to heartless ridicule.*

"How are you, John?" It was a simple question, and most people would answer it without a second thought. For me, it was torture.

I had just accepted a ride from one of my teachers. As I was getting into the backseat, his wife turned, smiled at me, and asked the question. Obviously she had not been warned. There was a quick exchange of looks in the front seat, but it was too late. The question had been asked, and it would have been rude to retract it.

If I had known this question awaited me, I may not have accepted the ride. But there it was, and I was obligated to respond. So I started giving my three-word answer.

For the next few minutes, a series of odd noises flowed out of my mouth. My face became contorted, while I slowly moved my head back and forth. The lady in the front seat just looked at me. She no longer smiled.

I finally ended the agony by saying, "Fine, thank you." The folks in the front seat then settled back and started visiting pleasantly with each other. I was left alone with my embarrassment.

OUT OF MY WEAKNESS

I have stuttered all my life. My family watched as I struggled to get one word to come out of my mouth. They tried everything to encourage me, but slowly I retreated into my own shell.

To make things worse, as a school-aged child I had serious learning problems. My teachers gave up hope for me academically. These disabilities made me an easy source of amusement for classmates.

At the same time, my father worked away from home for long periods of time and my parents were slowly moving toward a divorce. My mother watched helplessly as I struggled with these difficulties. She feared I would stop speaking altogether.

But then when I was sixteen, God stepped into this ruined life and worked a miracle of grace. I had been raised in a Bible-believing church, but somehow I had missed establishing a personal relationship with Jesus Christ. One Saturday afternoon, I bowed my head and yielded my life to His control. God brought light and hope into my dark place.

I basked in the Lord's life-changing presence for two years. Then God's Spirit impressed upon me that I was being called to preach. I thought it was just a crazy idea invading my thinking. I couldn't believe this "call" to public speaking was coming from God.

In time I came to realize God was calling me into a ministry that involved talking in front of people. This confused me because there were two obstacles. First, I was "educationally challenged." Those who wanted to be nice said, "John, you are not working up to your potential." Others tried to challenge me by saying, "You're just not trying." Classmates would laugh and call me the class dummy. God surely would not want to put someone like this on a speaker's platform. What could the "class dummy" say that anyone would want to hear?

The second obstacle was my inability to talk. *Hasn't God been listening?* I thought. *I can't talk.* Speaking had been next to impossible, and it had exposed me to heartless ridicule. I had learned to avoid this type of mockery at any cost. I knew standing up in front of a group of people, with the intent of saying anything, was an invitation for humiliation.

There was a spiritual motivation as well. I thought I was protecting the reputation of Christ. I was sure that making a fool of myself would not promote the cause of the gospel.

To protect myself, I had to turn down God's proposition. Over the next few months, I found God was not making a suggestion or giving me a proposal. It was a command. He wasn't giving me other options. There was no "plan B." I was perplexed because there was nothing in my experiences that matched up with what God was asking me to do.

FOLLOWING GOD'S LEADING

I spent months trying to reason with God about His calling for my life. I bargained, offered compromises, and even threatened. God was patient. All He wanted me to do was yield, which I finally did.

It occurred to me that God often tested people to prove their faith. He had no intention of allowing Abraham to sacrifice his son; He simply wanted a willing heart. I was confident that this must be what God was doing in my life. Surely He would never actually want someone who stuttered to become a public speaker.

I came up with a plan. I was in college and attended a church about an hour's drive from campus. I decided to ask the pastor if I could speak in a church service. I was confident he would say, "John, you know you can't talk. Your stuttering puts certain limitations on you. I am not going to give my pulpit to someone who stutters. You stay in the music department, and leave the preaching to me."

I would respond meekly, "I appreciate your wise counsel. I will try harder to accept myself the way God made me."

I could then go to God with the knowledge I had tried to become a public speaker, but it didn't work. It was a wonderful plan.

The next Sunday, I talked to the pastor after the morning service. I tried to make my stuttering sound as bad as I could. I asked if I could speak at a church service sometime. He cheerfully responded, "Sure. I'll put you down for next Sunday night."

THIS CAN'T BE HAPPENING TO ME

Next Sunday night! I stood dumbfounded as he walked off. What was he thinking? My plan had backfired. Not only did I lose a good excuse with God, but now I had to get up in front of the church and speak. I became frantic as I drove back to campus.

During the week, I remembered our pastor had a great sense of humor. Maybe he was just playing along with me to see how far I would go with this silly notion. Surely he knew it wasn't a good idea for me get up in front of the church and talk.

I went back the next Sunday with hope in my heart, but in the morning service he announced I was the speaker that evening.

That evening, it seemed the service had an extra big crowd. I am sure people were thinking, *This I've got to see.* I could imagine them talking afterward: "John got up and spoke for twenty minutes and said only three words."

I sat in the speaker's seat like a man awaiting execution. The song service passed too quickly. Soon the pastor was introducing me. I walked to the podium feeling like a martyr.

That is when it happened, and it has never happened to me since. I spoke for twenty-five minutes and did not stutter one time. It was as if God were telling me, "If I want you to do something, I will give you the ability to do it. Don't worry about what is possible. Your concern is to *obey* and *follow* My leading."

At the end of the sermon, I was amazed at what I had just experienced. I had never talked that long in my life without stuttering. Stepping off the platform, I spoke to someone and stuttered just as much as before. In good humor, I thought, *That's not fair. If I don't stutter behind the pulpit, why do I have to stutter down here?*

Today I talk before large audiences on a regular basis, and I stutter every time I stand up to speak. Through the years, my stuttering has decreased in severity, but God has never taken it away from me.

THIS BOOK IS FOR YOU

Can you identify with my story? Do your experiences contradict where God seems to be leading you? Even as you read this chapter, you may know God's voice is calling you to walk down a path, but you are unsure of your ability to do so.

If the Lord's leading involves your speaking in front of people, I can help. If God is "tapping on your shoulder" and you are apprehensive, this book is for you. I have been there, I know how you feel, and I can lead you through the exciting new adventure God has for you.

If I can speak before groups, you can too. I have already claimed all of the excuses. They belong to me. Since I own them, I can show you how to overcome them. In this book I will teach you some of the things God has taught me.

God has made me qualified to help inexperienced speakers, as well as seasoned veterans. I can help the first group because I know where I came from. I started off with no speaking advantages. I have had to develop these skills by yielding to God's leading.

I COULD NEVER DO THAT

If you cringe at the thought of speaking in front of a crowd, you probably wonder why you started reading this chapter. You remind me of Loretta. She couldn't believe she had let herself be talked into coming to one of my storytelling workshops. For years her pastor had tried to get her to teach a Sunday school class. She was willing to help with food preparation and art projects, but she would never consent to teaching a class. Now she found herself in a story-telling workshop.

I asked several people to tell the group why they came. Loretta said she wanted to do a better job of telling stories to her grandchildren. I think she wanted me to say, "That's not a good reason. If you don't plan to use this in a ministry, you will have to leave the class." Instead, the entire class thought learning to tell stories to grandchildren was a noble reason to be there.

I led the group through many activities. Each person was to prepare his or her own Bible story. During the last group activity of the day, I had several volunteers tell their stories in front of everyone. Loretta's partner was adamant that Loretta tell her story. Blushing, she got up and stood before the class. She did a masterful job with a story she called "Rachel and Her Biceps."

We smiled as she told us of a strong, determined young woman carrying bucket after bucket of water for thirsty camels. We laughed as we heard about this sweaty girl standing before Abraham's servant, while he put jewelry all over her. We were all moved as Loretta described Rachel's submission to the will of God. That day we heard a wonderful story of a brave young woman being asked to go and marry a young man in a far-off country. The applause was deafening.

I don't know if Loretta went back to her church and started teaching a Sunday school class. But I do know that she found storytelling fun and rewarding. She discovered that once she had learned a few simple steps, she could tell a fantastic story.

FOR THOSE ALREADY GOOD AT COMMUNICATING

If you are an experienced communicator, you may feel you can't improve. People already listen in rapt attention as you unfold the truths of God's Word. You are thinking, *How could I improve my skills?* This book is also for you. It will sharpen your communication skills to a new intensity.

After years of struggling with talking to crowds, there came a time when I realized I was a good public speaker. God had taught me to communicate, and my stuttering had become a trademark.

My brother-in-law, Gordon, asked me to speak at the church he pastored in Ohio. My wife and I traveled there, and I preached for him on Sunday. The next morning, in the middle of Wal-Mart, Gordon turned to me and said, "You ought to become a storyteller." I smiled because I was sure he was talking about entertaining children. I enjoyed speaking to adult audiences in churches, business seminars, student competitions, and teacher conferences. I wasn't interested in focusing on children's storytelling.

A year and a half later, at a New Year's Eve event, I heard a professional storyteller telling stories to adults. I sat enthralled and captivated. *Wow,* I thought. *I can do that. I want to do that.* I turned to my wife, but she spoke first since she doesn't stutter. "You could do that. You should do that."

I started going to storytelling festivals, conferences, and workshops. I learned from people who were not generally good at public speaking, but when they told stories, they were the masters and I was the student. It wasn't as easy as it seemed; still, I saw the potential. It has turned thick walls into open doors. I finally began to understand why our Lord didn't speak to the crowds except in stories (Matthew 13:34).

WHY BOTHER COMMUNICATING?

Maybe being a good communicator has never been your concern. You are gifted at digging out truths from the Word of God, but you have difficulty keeping the attention of your audience. You have always wondered why fellow Christians don't share your excitement about the deeper things of the Scriptures. "Oh well," you say, "my gifts lie in different areas." You would be embarrassed if anyone saw you reading a silly book on storytelling.

Don't put storytelling aside so easily. Keep reading. Your research will affect people in a greater way with just a few slight adjustments. You have too much to offer to allow the attention of your audience to wander from what you are saying.

AN ADDED BONUS

Recently my wife and I stopped for lunch as we were coming home from a vacation. The owner of the restaurant told me he had taken my course "Making a Bible Story Unforgettable." I asked if it had influenced the way he teaches his Sunday school class. He said, "Yes, it has changed the way I teach, and the way the teens in my class pay attention. It has even changed our family devotions. But that is not the most exciting part."

He paused and waited until he had my undivided concentration (using his newly acquired storytelling skills on me). Then he said slowly, "It has changed…the way I read the Bible.… John, I have been faithful at my devotions for years,…but now,…Scripture stories come alive to me in a new way."

YOUR TURN

Storytelling is a gift we all have. God has given you this gift, and it is superior to the storytelling ability given to any other earthly creature. I compare it to the gift of smell that God gave dogs. Some dogs have a keener sense of smell than others, but they all have it. The worst nose on a dog is still hundreds of times more sensitive than the best human nose.

Similarly, some people have developed their storytelling gifts to a higher level, but that doesn't change the fact that you already have tremendous storytelling abilities. Over the years you have been naturally improving your storytelling skills, and you would continue to do so—even without my help. Even so, stay with me.

Read this book, and do the exercises. Those who simply read every chapter at a normal level of comprehension will improve their skills. But those who study the book—and do the exercises—will increase their abilities, enjoyment, effectiveness, ministry, and the pleasure of those around them. The exercises are designed to offer you shortcuts that would take years to learn on your own.

I am praying God will use this book to expand the ministry He has given you. Pause and join me in this prayer. Ask Him to be your teacher as you do each exercise.

✳

You have too much to offer to allow the attention of your audience to wander from what you are saying.

✳

Chapter One

✱

A NEW WORLD AND ITS STORY

Enhancing your story-telling skills will increase your ability to affect people you have not been able to reach before.

It was a drizzly Sunday morning when my daughter Christie and her husband, Michael, were getting ready for church. Michael needed to stay home and take care of their two sons who were sick. He helped Christie get the two girls into the car, kissed them all good-bye, and they were off.

When the trio arrived at church, Christie delivered Amelia to the nursery and escorted Laura to children's church. She planted herself in the auditorium, finding pleasure in knowing she could enjoy the pastor's sermon without being distracted with restless children.

Christie always enjoyed the way her pastor preached with love and compassion. It was evident that he put a lot of preparation into his sermons; that Sunday was no different. She took notes, all the while thinking, *God has given our pastor such insight.*

When the service ended, Christie gathered her two daughters together, and the three headed home where the men of the family awaited them. Upon entering the house, Christie was greeted with a kiss from her husband, who asked how the service was.

"Great!" she replied with enthusiasm. She told him about the choir rehearsal after the service, and how she practiced her solo in preparation for the next Sunday.

"What was the sermon about?" asked Michael.

"Oh, um…well…it was really good." She wracked her brain for details of the sermon that had meant so much to her, but she couldn't remember a thing. She thought all the activity after the service caused her memory to lapse. Finally, she shuffled through her Bible where she recovered the notes she had taken.

"Let's see…" she said, her voice trailing off as she skimmed her notes. "Ah, yes. That's right. He was preaching on Luke. Remember? He's doing that series through the gospel of Luke. It was really good."

From behind her, Laura exclaimed, "I remember what Mr. Gorman spoke about in children's church." With that, the child went into enthusiastic detail about all her teacher had spoken about in the children's service. Not only did she remember the entire sermon, she was able to relate it in a way that made her parents wish they had been able to hear such an exciting presentation of the gospel.

Did my granddaughter remember the sermon because she is younger and has a better memory? Not at all. While preparing his lesson, Mr. Gorman was aware of how his audience receives and remembers information. This should be done whenever a presentation is prepared for any group.

Two types of adults respond especially well to stories. They are 1) *story thinkers* and 2) *men*. Knowing about these two groups will help you to adapt your lesson, sermon, or business presentation with them in mind.

ADAPTING PRESENTATIONS FOR STORY THINKERS

On September 11, 2001, four jet airliners were hijacked. Terrorists flew two of them into the twin towers in New York City, and the other two flew toward Washington, D.C. Our society, and life as we know it, has not been the same since.

That same afternoon, I was visiting with a professor friend of mine. He asked, "What do you think, John? How do you feel about what happened today?"

My answer was simple: "Well, everything has changed. I was used to life, just the way it was. I didn't want it to change, but it has." After a little pause, I added, "I wonder what the new world is going to be like."

Most people did not want the events of that day. It was tragic, and we didn't like it. Still, it happened, and we all had to adjust.

Our culture has gone through another change that also has altered our society. Many Christian ministries were not aware of it because of its low profile. Since they didn't know about it, they didn't make the needed adjustments. Other ministries knew about it but labeled it as ungodly, so they continued on as if everything were the same as it used to be.

What has happened, and how should we adjust to it? The difference is in the way people *receive* information and the way people *remember* information.

People of my generation are considered analytical thinkers. For us, everything is linear. We think in facts and figures, and the best way to communicate to us is through an outline.

If you want the analytical thinker to remember the information for any length of time, you create points and put them in order. For instance, you could make sure all the words of the outline start with the same letter. Better yet, have the first letter of all the points spell out a word.

It was not always necessary to include stories, unless, of course, they reinforced the outline. Stories were props that supported and illustrated the theme. Because of this, we stopped calling them stories and started calling them *illustrations.*

Sorry, but that has all changed. Most people born after the Baby Boomers receive information best in the form of stories. They are not linear; they are what I call *story thinkers.*

These people have become some of the most creative, productive citizens of our society. They want the information, and they want it straight. But they want it in a way that holds their interest. Stories are the best way to reach this new breed of thinker. They are left cold if you try to impress them with outlines or by putting your main points in some order. You still need a theme and even an outline; just don't let them know you have it. They don't want your clever tricks and ingenious alliterations.

TIME TO ADJUST

I went to a Christian school several years ago to teach creative writing to their students. The principal was concerned about my going into one particular fourth grade class. The teacher had tried everything but was frustrated. The principal told me, "The class is full of problem students. I predict you will have difficulty there."

He felt it wise to accompany me, and I was glad for his reinforcement. As I taught the class, he sat in the back, amazed. I was using storytelling to teach the students to create, write, and rewrite. He watched as these students listened in rapt attention. He was astonished at how I kept the room in seeming chaos, yet every student was learning and creating. Students walked around the room, sat on the floor, talked to one another, participated in fun activities, and created fantastic compositions. This classroom was full of story-thinking students, and I was successful with them because I adjusted to their way of thinking. It seemed chaotic, but it was organized and completely under my control.

THE SCRIPTURES CONTAIN BOTH

Jesus stood before Galileans and looked into their faces. He had a message and wanted them to listen and remember what He said. He opened His mouth and told them stories. People say Jesus was the master teacher because of His use of stories. No, He was the master teacher because He knew His audience and adapted His message to their way of thinking.

Paul stood before Greeks and looked into their faces. He had a message and wanted them to listen and remember what he said. He opened his mouth and used analytical reasoning to explain the gospel. He knew his audience and adapted his presentation.

Later, when Paul went to Jerusalem, he neglected to adapt his presentation for the Jewish audience. When he used the analytical method that worked so well with his Gentile audience, the people standing before him were unmoved by his message. Only the Romans listened to him.

Many today are making the same mistake. We should always present God's Word in a way that is consistent with how people think.

The Bible reflects the different ways in which people receive and remember information. The various writers of Scripture wrote to either story or analytical thinkers. The Gospels are written in stories. To this day, they appeal to the story thinkers in our society. The Epistles are analytical and appeal to that type of thinker. Both need to be read and studied, but the appeal is different.

It is no longer acceptable to add an illustration near the end of a lesson, sermon, or business presentation. Storytelling techniques provide you with the ability to skillfully adjust your message so that you are talking the language of the people around you. Today your audience thinks in stories, they remember stories, and they will listen if you tell stories.

A few years ago, I was teaching a storytelling workshop in a church in Waterloo, Iowa. Afterwards, a lady told me she enjoyed learning how to tell stories, but she had a problem. She was scheduled to speak to a group of people that next week, and they were going to allow her only seven minutes. She wanted to know, "How can I give my three important points and still have time to tell a story?"

My answer was *not* to add an illustration to her points. I showed her how to create a seven-minute story that contained all three concepts she wanted to communicate. The key was to emphasize the story and not the points. I said, "Your talk will be the most dramatic seven minutes of the day, and the audience will never forget it." The solution to her predicament illustrates the change in our society.

ADAPTING YOUR PRESENTATION FOR MEN AND WOMEN

A second group of people responds especially well to stories. Generally speaking, there is a difference in how men and women receive information. Men tend to think in pictures, while women tend to think in words.

I was in a meeting of business people attended mostly by men. A woman came to talk about her business. She spent the entire time telling us all the facts concerning her exciting work. Unfortunately, she was talking words, not pictures. While no one physically left the room, all of the men slipped out mentally. They kept their bodies in the meeting to be polite. Each one started thinking about things unrelated to what she was talking about.

I knew this lady had fantastic stories that would have completely captivated this group. She just wasn't using them. Instead, she was reasoning with the group, trying to enlist their encouragement and support.

I knew her well enough to feel I could talk to her about the situation. I also knew she would appreciate knowing why she didn't sway her audience in a way that would move them to action.

I waited a few days and made an appointment with her. I asked how she felt the meeting went. She knew all had not gone well but was puzzled.

When she asked my opinion, I explained about the different thinking processes of men and women. I told her to relate stories instead of giving facts the next time she gave a presentation to men. I asked a series of questions to find out what was important to communicate to such a group of business people. I should have gotten all this at the meeting, but being a man, I guess I wasn't listening.

I asked her to tell me a set of stories that illustrated all her information. Together, we put her points inside the stories. Soon we had created a presentation about herself, her clients, and the impact her business was making. It transformed how she was received in the business community. She was able to tell all the facts, but now they were hidden in interesting stories. Not only did her audience pay attention, but everyone remembered what she said.

A Group Exercise

---

* Ask someone in the group to tell about a job, business, ministry, or profession. This will work especially well if you select someone who is preparing for an upcoming presentation.

* Have that person give three or four aspects that are important concerning this job, business, ministry, or profession.

* Have him/her tell a story (in no more than two minutes) that illustrates each area.

* Weave these stories together to make a formal presentation. The presentation should not be longer than ten minutes.

REACHING LISTENERS WITH YOUR STORY

We are called to minister to both *analytical* and *story thinkers.* We are to communicate to both men and women.

You may need to create stories designed to enhance business presentations or influence clients. You may want to specialize in children's stories for your Sunday school class or children's church. Perhaps you sense a need to put a new spark into family devotions and capture the hearts of your children. It may be that you want to become more creative in the way you prepare and present sermons.

This book may just increase your ability to impact those you may have been unable to reach until now. This book will teach you to prepare a story and present it in a way that leaves a lasting impression.

If you learn and use these skills:

- Children will focus on what you are teaching.
- Adults will pay attention to your message.
- You will improve your relationship with professional clients.
- Family members will enjoy family devotions.

- Church members will remember what was taught.
- Nonbelievers may finally understand the gospel.

GOOD NEWS, BAD NEWS

Learning to connect with story thinkers is easy compared to communicating with analytical thinkers. The only reason many of us like the old way better is because that is what we are used to.

Read this manual (more than once), practice each simple step, and do all the exercises. It is going to show you how to prepare and tell stories that story thinkers will hear and remember. The men and boys in your audience will listen with a higher level of attention.

Unfortunately, Christians are a little behind in this area. For years the world has been teaching humanistic philosophy in story form. Theaters, books, music, television, and videos have perfected the art of concealing teaching inside stories. Even news broadcasts have changed to a series of stories. Still, we can make up for lost time. Follow these steps, learn the skills, and reach out to a world that is desperate for your message.

*

Before, people heard you speak.
Now, they will understand what you are saying.

*

FOURTEEN STEPS TO PREPARING AN UNFORGETTABLE STORY

✳

Those who present an unforgettable story have taken time to prepare an unforgettable story. The following fourteen steps will equip you to prepare a story that will hold an audience captive.

Chapter Two

✳

"WHERE DO YOU FIND YOUR STORIES?"

> *Few things are as exciting as creating a story that is all your own.*

Let's say you have been asked to tell a story for the adult Sunday school summer cookout. This starts the search for *the perfect story.* You rummage around, read books, ask for help from friends, but all to no avail. You finally give up on finding *the perfect story.* Any old one will have to do.

We have heard wonderful stories all our lives, and some of them are dear to us. The world is full of stories, yet we can't find one that fits both the occasion and us. The search can be frustrating.

I am going to simplify the "finding" process for you, but I must ask you to be patient. It may require you to take a couple of steps back before you are able to move forward. No matter how experienced you are at public speaking, I recommend you move in sequence through the following three levels of stories.

LEVEL 1: START WITH LEARNER STORIES

You may already have command of the platform, but storytelling requires different skills. Few public speakers have taken the time to improve their ability to relate a story skillfully.

I have a friend who is a retired drama professor at a local state university. He has written, acted in, and directed live dramatic productions for years. I encouraged him to go into story-telling. Although he used his experience and knowledge, he still had to start in this new arena with the basics.

Possibly you are a beginner at platform work. Don't be unnerved by the fact that you are developing this skill next to seasoned platform professionals. Don't try to keep up with someone else, and don't compare your progress with others. This manual is designed to explain everything carefully and not to assume knowledge on the part of the reader. I recommend that you plan to work through this book several times.

After you complete the process, you may feel you need to stay with "learner stories" for a while longer. If so, I recommend getting a *Ready to Tell* book. These are written in a *telling* format rather than a *reading* format. They also contain hints and suggestions in the margins. I have included the titles of several *Ready to Tell* books in the resource section in the appendix of this manual.

Once you have mastered a few learner stories, you will be ready to move to the next level. Have patience; eventually you will be developing perfect stories, tailor-made for your ministry.

LEVEL 2: TRIED AND PROVEN

The next level of stories is "old favorites." Over the years these have been perfected and come down to us as classics. They are fun stories you enjoy telling at family get-togethers, office functions, or church fellowships.

You will find a limited list of these in the resource section of this manual. Another way to find old favorites is to listen to other storytellers. Select one of their fictional tales, and ask for permission to use it. This book will teach you how to adjust it so that it fits your personality.

One of the best ways to find these "classics" is to talk to the librarians in the children's department of your public library. They love to be asked for recommendations. Call them in advance and tell them you are developing your storytelling skills. Ask if they can help you find books that contain "old standbys." When you go to their department in the library, no doubt they will have a stack of books waiting for you.

LEVEL 3: CREATING NEW STORIES FROM EXISTING ONES

Once you have practiced with old favorites, you will want to move on to the third level. This will open the door to an endless source of stories.

The world is full of great stories someone else has taken the time to create. They have followed certain established rules of development. In most cases, you are permitted to change them to fit your personality and situation. In doing this, there are two precautions:

- Generally, you are at liberty to tell someone's fictional story as long as you are not being paid to do so, and you are not making a salable recording of it. If you are planning to do either of these, contact the author and ask for written permission.

- Many Native American stories were created as part of a religious ceremony. In respect to their culture, it is best not to retell these stories out of that setting.

PROCESS FOR CHANGING A STORY

Recently I was asked to tell a story at our church's Thanksgiving service. There were three requirements. It was to be about twenty minutes long, have a Thanksgiving theme, and contain a good Christian message. "Oh, by the way," the pastor added, "try to make it enjoyable."

My pastor wanted to add a little variety to the traditional service. It was my job to help him do it. I had to find a story that would be just right for this occasion. There is a world of possibilities that could be used. What type of tale should I look for? Here are the criteria I use when I search for a story.

LESS IS BETTER

Start with a small story. It doesn't matter if your presentation is to be ten minutes or forty-five minutes; it is always best to start with a smaller story. The reason is simple: you must major on being descriptive if you want a story to be gripping and unforgettable.

Even when approaching a Bible story, look for a short one. If the scriptural account is long, create a story from a small section of it. An illustration of this is the life of Joseph. I tell a series of stories that cover the life of Joseph that would take over an hour and a half if I told them all at one time.

You want your listeners to relate the story to specific needs in their lives. Starting with a smaller story allows you time to make it relevant to the culture and feelings of your audience. Later we'll learn to expand it to fill the time allotment.

THE RESOURCE OF CHILDREN'S BOOKS

As I searched for a Thanksgiving story, I visited the children's department of my local library. I called my favorite children's librarian and said, "Georgianne, do you have any Thanksgiving stories?" She selected several that she especially liked and put them aside for me, saving me an enormous amount of work. If I had chosen to search for a story by myself, I might have gone through a hundred books to find the one I wanted.

Asking for the help of professionals saves time and frustration. Also, it is a compliment to them. Books are their life and area of expertise. Be sure to thank them for their help. They are a storyteller's best friend.

Children's books are the best source for small, well-structured stories. Books written for adults are full of details that entertain a reader but get in the way of a storyteller. In Appendix 1, I will show you how to take an adult short story and develop it for telling. For now, though, children's books are your best source for thousands of stories.

A QUALITY STORY

Once I arrived at the library, I looked at the seven books Georgianne had selected. Now it was time to decide which story was the best for the occasion and for me. Each person is different, so you will need to determine what is important to you. I look for two qualities and two qualities only:

DO I LIKE THE STORY?

I would not be able to exude excitement before an audience if I did not like the story myself. Besides, once I have developed the story, I will tell it to many audiences for years. Eventually, it becomes a close friend, so it is important that I like it initially.

DO I LIKE THE ENDING?

I can change the rest of the story to fit the occasion and my personality, but good endings are hard to find. I consider a good ending a nonnegotiable element. Many storytellers have no problem with this. They are willing to have a flat ending as long as they have good substance in the middle. Again, you must establish what is important to you.

MAKING APPROPRIATE CHANGES

I found a story that had both qualities, and I was able to change it to fit the special service.

To clarify further, let me illustrate how these two qualities helped me prepare for another occasion. I was asked to tell a cowboy story for the Museum of History. I could not find one I liked in the short amount of time I had. Suddenly, I came across a Japanese story that had a great plot and a wonderful ending. Before I had finished working on it, the little family in the story no longer lived in Japan. They lived in western Wyoming in the late 1800s. Jim was trying to get his herd established, and Helen was making a home out of a sod-roofed cabin. Their daughter was unaware she was isolated from civilization; instead, she made friends with local "Indians." Most important, she had a vivid imagination. The story fit the occasion and has delighted many audiences since.

THE RED FLAG OF MEMORIZING

While I am talking about selecting and preparing stories, I must pause here and wave a red flag about memorized stories. New storytellers will think, *I want to make sure I say everything just right. I don't want to leave anything out.* These are legitimate concerns, but memorizing is not the solution. There are several disadvantages of memorized stories.

MEMORIZING LIMITS STORYTELLING

It is important for a storyteller to constantly develop new material. You may be able to commit a few stories to memory, but eventually you are going to reach your limit. Also, a memorized story has to be continually reviewed or it will be lost. You will not run out of room in your brain, but you may run out of time for all the rehearsals.

MEMORIZING LIMITS FLEXIBILITY

A freestyle story is one that is not memorized and can be adapted for different audiences. These changes may come in the middle of a presentation. Several times I started to recite a memorized story, only to quickly realize it was not going well. If it had been a freestyle story, I could have made some quick adjustments, but as it was, I was stuck.

Flexibility is more valuable than the false security you might feel by memorizing the story.

MEMORIZING DOESN'T PROTECT YOU

There may be some good reasons to memorize a story, but security is not one of them. Freestyle storytelling has drawbacks. There will be times when you leave something out that should have been said. At other times, you will say the wrong words, and people will look at you with puzzled expressions on their faces. (Recently I told a story in which I had the main character guiding his boat with an "udder" rather than a "rudder.")

Still, forgetting things in a freestyle story will usually go unnoticed. The story will stand on its own, without those statements you thought were so important. But when you go blank and forget memorized lines, it usually stops everything. And believe me, no matter how well you have a story memorized, you *will* forget your lines at one time or another.

I tell three stories that are memorized. I have quoted these stories for years and have rehearsed them on a regular basis. No one on this planet knows the lines better than I do. Still, on occasion, I forget the words in the middle of a performance. I know this will happen; yet I stubbornly want to tell the stories anyway. Each time I begin to tell one of these, I acknowledge the fact that this could be another time that I forget the lines. I have prepared myself for a lapse of memory so I know what to do when it happens. Even so, forgetting lines is not pleasant.

MEMORIZING MAY DISTRACT FROM MINISTRY

The ultimate goal of those in any Christian ministry is to focus on people and their needs. The focus of a storyteller should be on the message and the response of the audience. Memorizing a story often turns the focus toward words—making sure they are correct. The performance often becomes story-centered rather than audience-centered.

MEMORIZING MAKES YOU LESS "COPYABLE"

You may have the skills to overcome all of these obstacles and be good at preparing and presenting memorized stories. This is a rare talent, and you should use it. Just keep this thought in mind: each person in a Christian ministry is to encourage others to get involved and join the work of the Lord.

Every time I give a memorized story, I hear, "I could never do that." But when I tell a freestyle story, people come up afterward and ask how they can improve their own skills. They want to learn more about storytelling. They feel they can do it. The principle is this: however you serve the Lord, make sure it encourages others to do the same. In other words, be "reproducible."

SIMPLY TELL THE STORY

It may be hard to imagine yourself standing in front of an audience and telling a story without having every word planned out. You may think if it is not memorized, you will at least need notes. Believe me, these are not necessary. You will learn to stand and simply tell a story without security props. And you'll have fun doing it.

Don't rush ahead and memorize something. Learn your stories in a way that will flow naturally, and they will be ready whenever opportunity presents itself.

Now we are ready to take the first of the fourteen steps in preparing a story.

STEP 1:
Select a Story

It is time to select a story. I am going to assign you a preselected story for us to work on together. I want you to select a second one from the list below. Ten of them are Bible stories, and the other five are stories you can find in Appendix 2 of this manual. Choose one you have not told in front of a group.

- Laughing at God . . . . .Genesis 18:9–15
- Rebekah and the Camels . . . . .Genesis 24:10–28
- A Distressed Mother . . . . .1 Kings 17:17–24
- Wrestling with God . . . . .Genesis 32:22–32
- Moses and the Ark . . . . .Exodus 2:1–10
- Moses at the Well . . . . .Exodus 2:15–22
- "Read My Lips" . . . . .1 Samuel 1:2–19
- Hearing the Voice of God . . . . .1 Samuel 3:1–10
- Bread and Oil . . . . .1 Kings 17:8–16
- Hem of the Garment . . . . .Luke 8:43–48
- *The Lonely Shepherd Boy* . . . . .Appendix 2, p. 177
- *The Donkey's Impressive Attire* . . . . . .Appendix 2, p. 178
- *A Girl and Her Dreams* . . . . .Appendix 2, p. 178
- *Father, Son, and Donkey* . . . . .Appendix 2, p. 179
- *Big Friend, Little Friend* . . . . .Appendix 2, p. 180

The preselected story that we will work on together is called "Noah and the Birds" from Genesis 8:6–13. I have selected this passage because of its difficulty level. As you read the verses in Genesis, you will see it would be difficult to make it into a story, especially if you were limited to just this section of Scripture. As you learn to develop this difficult story, you will be able to transfer the same step-by-step procedure to the second story you have selected.

Once you have taken these steps, you are ready to move to the next chapter.

Learn your stories in a way that will flow naturally, and they will be ready whenever opportunity presents itself.

---

t i m e   t o   p r a c t i c e

✳ Before you start the next chapter, read "Noah and the Birds" in Genesis 8:6–13. Be sure you have selected a second story from the list provided. The next few steps will be meaningful to you only if you are in the story-construction process.

Chapter Three

✳

LET THEM WALK IN YOUR SHOES

> *I didn't know, until she told me, that Noah almost forgot to take the bucket on the trip. That would have been a miserable trip.*

The flickering fireplace looked so inviting, displaying colorful hues of orange and yellow. I leaned back in my easy chair, listening to the crackle and hiss of burning wood and enjoying the faint smell of smoke. It added warmth to a cold winter evening and offered comfort at the end of a hectic day.

A good story would be the perfect complement to this cozy setting. I was in the mood for one that came from the Old Testament, so I picked up the Bible and turned on the side lamp. The page fell open to 2 Kings 4. My eyes skimmed to verses 38–41, which had the heading, "Elisha heals the noxious pottage."

I read the passage several times to make sure I understood what was recorded about this incident. I wondered if it were part of a greater series of events, so I read the few chapters that came before. They added little additional light on what happened. The account stood by itself.

Although I had no intention of telling this in front of an audience, I took the story to step two without a second thought. I wanted to gain a better understanding of what might have happened that day. In fact, in my mind I walked through all the steps in this chapter.

When I finished reading, I turned off the lamp and looked into the flickering fire, watching the story unfold before my eyes. The prophet Elisha and his small group of men camped in the mountain region of Gilgal. Several of them had gone out to gather provisions for a meal. I walked with a young man who found some gourds that were poisonous. Without asking, he went back to the fire, took out his knife, and shredded them into the stew.

I was there. It was convenient that my fire was a lot like theirs. The drama unfolded before me: the pot of stew on the open fire, the poison that contaminated the precious food, and the miracle of the servant of God.

Now we'll discover how to bring a story like this one to life. The added benefit of all this story development is that you just may find a fresh way to enliven your private devotions.

 STEP 2:
Pushing Through the Story

This step is simple but critical. Once you have read the story several times, put the book away and talk through it. Tell it to another person—or merely tell it to a chair, bookshelf, or another object in the room. The important part is to talk completely through the story. You are not performing at this point but simply telling what you know about it.

I prefer telling the story to someone. My wife is usually kind enough to listen as I go through this process. Recently my grown son has been stopping by for this purpose. We call it our "exchange program." I listen to his story, and he listens to mine.

Pushing through a story does several things.

- It takes the story off the written page and puts it into a *telling* form. This is an informal telling of the story, and you don't have it memorized, so don't worry about getting all the details correct at this point.

- It helps you see if you have all the *important* facts straight in your memory. While you don't need to remember all the details, the structure does need to be in place.

- It gives you a chance to see if you enjoy telling the story. Simply reading it does not provide you this gauge. Sometimes I like reading a story, but it goes flat once I tell it. Other times a story will seem dull when I read it, but it comes alive when I tell it.

Storytelling is an art form best developed in front of people. Telling a story is the only time you can get a true feel of its quality. It allows you an opportunity to hear yourself as you tell it.

PUTTING THE CLAY ON THE WHEEL

I compare this step to putting potter's clay onto the wheel. Before the potter can create a sculptured piece of art, he must remove the clay from its bucket and put it onto the table or wheel.

By pushing through a story, you are taking a written narrative and putting it into your mind. It is raw and undeveloped, but it has potential. To simply think about the story without telling it is like looking at the clay in the bucket. It just doesn't get the job done. Take the story out of the bucket, push through it, and listen to yourself tell it.

---

time to practice

✳ Read Genesis 8:6–13 two or three times, and then close your Bible and talk through it. Make it simple, yet as detailed as possible without rereading the story. After you have completed this step, read the story one more time.

A Group Exercise

✳ Allow each person time to read Genesis 8:6–13.

✳ Ask for a volunteer to stand and push through the story for the group.

✳ Allow others to add more details to the story that the volunteer may have left out.

---

t i m e   t o   p r a c t i c e

✳ Now let's work on the story you have selected. Read it several times and once you are ready, put it aside and push through it.

A Group Exercise

✳ Divide the class into groups of two and designate which person is number 1 and which is number 2.

✳ It is important that the 1s and 2s are working on different stories.

✳ Allow the 1s two minutes to tell their story to the 2s.

✳ At the end of two minutes, reverse roles.

✳ The job of a listener is to look at the person telling the story *and* appear interested with nods and sounds.

MOVE AWAY FROM THE BOOK

You'll do this first telling with no prompting or external support. Once you have pushed through a story, and reread it once more, you should not look back at the book.

If you are unsure of the structure of the plot, you may find you have to read the text several more times. If so, restart the entire process. Once you are ready, push through the story again; this time, don't look back. You will reread the story at a later time. For now, it is important to move away from the written format and begin shaping the spoken format.

STEP 3:
Envision the Scene with Present-Day Feelings and Concerns

You may want to research the Bible story at this point. This is not the time to do that. Wait until step ten. It is true that the study of Bible customs and times is useful in Bible story-telling. So much has been learned about ancient times, and these studies are now available to the average person. This information will make your story more intriguing, and we will use these insights when we take step ten. For now, such a study would interfere with making the story unforgettable.

People around the world look and act the same in many ways, but little dissimilarities stand out: customs, thinking, and traditions. Even people of our own culture who lived just a hundred years ago are different from us today. To understand what they were thinking and feeling would be impossible. Now add two or three millennia to the equation. Any attempt to get inside the minds of Bible people will necessarily require some creativity on our parts. No one truly knows the feelings and concerns people in Bible events were experiencing.

IN YOUR SHOES

The best-told Bible stories come to be when we tailor our stories to relate to people who feel, think, act, react, and talk just like we do. The way we adapt a biblical story is likely to have the greatest influence on people who live near us and are a part of our culture.

Your audience may be interested in a few facts about people in old times, but what they really want to know is, "Does the Bible relate to what I am going through now?" Yes. The Scripture does relate to our lives. It was written for us personally and is applicable to what we are going through.

The purpose of step three is to allow the Bible characters to *walk in your shoes*. They should think like you and feel what the members of your Bible study feel. In your story, they have the same concerns, heartaches, and frustrations that reign in your Sunday school class.

Once you are able to see these ancient people *in your shoes,* you can watch as they walk in the direction God leads them. This will help your listeners see what it is like to follow God. The story will come alive because it relates to real-life situations.

AT THE SCENE

The following exercise is one I call "At the Scene." It is great for family devotions or a small group Bible study. If you do it alone, I recommend you sit back in a relaxed position. When I do it, I often dim the lights and lean back in my chair.

First, let's do the exercise with "Noah and the Birds."

---

t i m e   t o   p r a c t i c e

* Picture yourself standing in the boat with Noah and his family. They can't see you, but you can see everything going on. In fact, you can feel what they are feeling, and you know what they are thinking. Noah has not yet sent out the first bird. As you stand there on the ark, answer the following questions and don't worry about accuracy. We will deal with that later. At this point, set aside what you don't know about the Noah family, and think about what may have been true. Take your time with each question.

A Group Exercise

* Ask each of the following questions, and allow the class enough time to discuss it thoroughly.

- Look around the boat and describe what you see.
- Who are the people there? Describe each one.
- Describe the sounds you hear.
- What do you smell?
- What relationships did each person leave behind?
- Name some of the chores that need to be done.

- Describe the various feelings, attitudes, and moods.
  (Be realistic, these were not perfect people.)
- What memories are influencing their thinking?
- How are the different personalities reacting to the situation, and to each other?
- Describe how the animals are enduring the trip.
- Describe the scene outside the boat.
- How do the people react to the various changes in weather?

---

time to practice

* Once you have thought through each of these questions, tell "Noah and the Birds" aloud without looking at the Bible or notes. Add in as much of the feelings and concerns as you can. You can tell it to someone or simply to the air around you.

A Group Exercise

* Ask 1s to tell the story to their 2s.

* After this, rearrange the groups so that every 1 has a different 2.

* Then reverse roles.

YOU'RE ON THE SCENE

Telling the story at this point gives you a chance to better understand the development process. You probably have a tremendous story already, but be patient; it is not close to finished yet.

Now it is time to put yourself at the scene of the story you have selected.

── *t i m e   t o   p r a c t i c e* ──

✳ You may copy the "At the Scene" worksheet at the end of this chapter for personal use. The questions are general. Use them as a starting point, but quickly move on to specific questions that relate directly to your story. The goal is to think through all the feelings and concerns of the people involved.

A Group Exercise

✳ Have the 1s ask "At the Scene" questions of the 2s (worksheet at the end of this chapter).

✳ Encourage them to move to more specific questions that better relate to the story.

✳ After five minutes, reverse roles.

Most of the sights, sounds, smells, and descriptions that come to mind never will be mentioned when you tell the story. It is only important that you have a clear picture of the situation from your life perspective.

── *t i m e   t o   p r a c t i c e* ──

✳ Once you have thought through the scene, tell the story to someone or even to a stuffed animal. Put in as many of the feelings and concerns as you can.

A Group Exercise

✳ Rearrange the groups so everyone is sitting with a different partner.

✳ Have each person tell his story to his new partner.

You are beginning to bring life to the story, because you are making it relevant to your culture. Still, there is much more to perfecting it.

STEP 4:
Tell the Story from the View of Someone at the Scene

With step three, you tried to think of feelings and concerns present during the incident. Now you will hear about it from someone who was there. This exercise will help you understand from a first-person viewpoint what it was like in the story.

I do not intend for you to tell the story this way when you stand in front of your audience. This step is just an exercise. You *may* choose to tell it this way, but that is a decision you will make down the road.

The Bible tells Genesis 8:6–13 from the narrator's viewpoint. Instead, try putting yourself into the story and telling it in the first person. It doesn't have to be a person. The purpose is to be objective, so you may want to hear from one of the animals or from an object nearby.

---

time to practice

* Imagine you are someone or something in the story. Possibly Noah, Mrs. Noah, or God. You might want to tell it from the viewpoint of one of the sons or maybe one of the daughters-in-law. Or an animal. How do they view all that is going on? Could the ark or some object on board have an opinion?

* Stand, even if you are alone, and tell the story as if you were that person, animal, or object.

A Group Exercise

✳ Ask everyone to choose a viewpoint but keep it secret until asked.

✳ Once everyone has made a choice, go around the room and have each tell what viewpoint she has chosen.

✳ Have the 1s stand and tell the story to the 2s from their chosen viewpoint; then reverse roles.

✳ Once everyone is finished, ask who just heard a fantastic story and would be willing to volunteer their partner to tell it to the group.

In one workshop, a lady told the whole story from the bucket's viewpoint. I didn't know, until she told me, that Noah almost forgot to take the bucket on the trip. That would have been a disastrous—not to mention miserable—trip.

I have heard a story told by a camel standing nearby. No one noticed him as he stood there with his nose in the air, but he saw all that was going on.

As silly as this may seem, it brings out a side of the trip that was real to the people on the boat. That's the purpose of this exercise: get yourself into the story and live with what they had to live with.

Although I go through this exercise personally, rarely do I keep the first person perspective when I tell a story to an audience. Most of my stories are told from the narrator's viewpoint. Still, when I narrate, that first person has a way of "speaking up" every now and then. I may be telling how Jesus healed a blind man, when suddenly a disciple speaks up and gives his perspective. This adds a spice to the story that makes it more real and enjoyable to the audience.

When you develop a story from a children's book, you often will find it written from a child's or an animal's point of view. That means someone already has gone through this exercise and has elected to keep the perspective. When doing this exercise with a children's book, tell the story in yet a different way. You may want to tell it from the narrator's viewpoint.

time to practice

* Now that you have practiced with "Noah and the Birds," put yourself into the story you have selected. Choose a major character or one of the casually mentioned "other people." Or put yourself in the character of a servant or neighbor who is not mentioned at all.

By doing all these exercises, you have started to develop quite a story. In the next chapter you will add the part that will make it unforgettable.

*

The best-told Bible stories come to be when we tailor our stories to relate to people who feel, think, act, react, and talk just like we do.

*

AT THE SCENE

1. Look around and describe what you see.

_____

_____

_____

_____

2. Who are the main characters? What do they look like?

_____

_____

_____

3. Describe the sounds and smells that are there.

_____

_____

_____

4. What other types of people could be in the area?

_____

_____

_____

_____

5. How do you think they are reacting to the situation at hand?

_____

_____

_____

_____

6. What memory or prejudice is influencing their thinking?

_____

_____

Chapter Four

✳

MAKE IT UNFORGETTABLE

> *The issue is not one of right/wrong, acceptable/unacceptable, or good/bad. The issue is forgettable/unforgettable.*

She cleared her throat and struggled to find the right words. The question had caught Julie off guard. She, along with several others from the women's Bible study, had attended a ladies' retreat. Now they were sharing their experience with the others in the group.

Julie had no problem telling about the fellowship she enjoyed and the new friends she had made. Everyone laughed when she excitedly described the water balloon fight. She explained how the special music and workshops had blessed her heart.

Suddenly, the leader of the Bible study asked her if she had attended the workshop titled "Seven Easy Steps to Walking in the Spirit," by Ethel Simian.

"Why yes, I did," she said hesitantly. She didn't want to admit she had almost fallen asleep in that session.

"I went to college with Ethel; she is such a dear lady. Tell us a little about her session."

Julie's mind raced to think of at least one thing the speaker had said. She finally dodged the question by excitingly telling about another workshop titled "Reflecting His Image." "It was wonderful. The speaker was a pastor's wife from Montana, and she told real-life experiences that had us laughing one minute and in tears the next." Before Julie was able to catch herself, she told the group about the entire workshop. She didn't answer the leader's question, but she did increase the ladies' interest in attending next year's retreat.

Why did Julie remember one workshop in its entirety, yet couldn't recall one statement from the other? It's simple. The pastor's wife from Montana had applied all three of the following steps to her workshop. These are the little secrets that make a big difference when you want your sermon, story, presentation, or speech *unforgettable.*

Why is this crucial? You may have only one opportunity to influence an individual or a group of people for eternity. Most of those who hear you speak will not respond to your message immediately, and many you will never see again. Therefore, you need to make a lasting impression. Later in their lives, they will come to a point where they have to make an important decision. Your goal is for the godly principles you taught to return to their minds.

Most people think the key to an unforgettable speech is good preparation, fervent prayer, and tremendous content. These are essential. But we all have heard sermons, Bible lessons, and stories that were well prepared and had tremendous content, yet we've forgotten what the speaker said within an hour.

STEP 5:
Establish the Story's One Central Truth

Storytellers often make one of two mistakes: either the story is devoid of any theme, or it is overloaded with lessons. The first step in making a story unforgettable is to establish one central truth in the story.

A story in its purest form does not overtly assert its central truth. This theme is only clearly stated if it is part of a lesson or sermon. Given by itself, the story stands without explanation.

Still, for it to make a lasting impression upon listeners, it should have a definite theme. When we hear a story with no apparent reason, we forget it quickly.

There is also the opposite extreme. Mike's job is to tell the Bible story in children's church. He is thrilled when he sees a visiting young man come into the room. He realizes he may have only one chance to influence this new visitor for the Lord. Seasoned pastors often joke about what Mike does at that point: "He starts at *Generations* and moves to *Revolutions*." He gives the class all he knows about meeting God, living for Him, and looking for His glorious return. The visitor walks out of class with his head spinning—forgetting the story, the class, and Mike.

What should Mike do? When preparing a story, he should ask himself, "What central truth does God want me to communicate today?" This will control how the plot is prepared and told. When Mike presents the story, the central truth will dominate it.

ACCEPTABLE VS. UNFORGETTABLE

The issue is not one of right/wrong, acceptable/unacceptable, or good/bad. The issue is forgettable and unforgettable. You can ignore this step and still be a good storyteller. You may tell a story that has no meaning or one that covers all the truths of the Bible. It is acceptable, but it will usually fall short of being unforgettable.

For a story to become powerful and lodge itself in the memories of the listeners, it must have one central truth and only one. You tell the story, and the story communicates the truth.

MAKE THE CENTRAL TRUTH POINTED

Think of the one truth that you want to emphasize with "Noah and the Birds." To determine that focus, ask yourself these questions: What one truth do I want to communicate to my listeners? Why would I take the time to tell this story? Why is it important? The answer to these questions becomes the theme.

The theme does not have to be life changing. I tell a simple story to teach that imagination can comfort you in stormy times. I never vocalize those words, and I am sure no one thinks them when I have finished. Still, the theme is there, and it influences the flow of the story. The story does its job even as I walk away.

Your central theme is best if it is specific. Rather than choosing a theme that says, "We need to have more faith in God," "Trust God at all times," or "Endure hardships," change these statements so they tell what Noah's faith did for him, or what was involved in trusting, or how endurance changed Noah. Good themes will sound more like:

> *Faith that ran contrary to experience*
> *Learning to trust while being confused*
> *Endurance turns frustrations into faith*

Any of these statements could be the underlying truth the story conveys. Notice: each of these would change the way the story is told.

Here, then, is the process I'd recommend: First, choose one truth to emphasize. Then, write it out so it becomes clear in your mind. Finally, brainstorm about how this theme will influence your telling of the story.

So far, you have told your selected story several times. Has an obvious theme surfaced? Let's practice writing a theme for the story you've selected.

A Group Exercise

✳ Choose one of the stories selected by a member of the group.

✳ Brainstorm and write several themes that could be taught by the story.

✳ Assign volunteers to tell the story, each using a different theme.

✳ Make the presentation short. The purpose is not to hear a polished story, but to see how its theme will change how it is told.

✳ Whether you're working with a group or on your own, now is the time to write your theme on paper so you can develop it easily. If you didn't have the benefit of participating in the group exercise described above, try to think of a different theme someone else might have chosen. Consider how that would change your telling of the story.

STEP 6:
Find a Memory Hook

A memory hook is a phrase, song, concept, or attitude repeated throughout the story. It is not the theme but simply a memory helper. Developing a memory hook may be the hardest step in the process. Don't be discouraged if you find this process challenging. For now it is important that you know about the principle. Once you know about it, you will start to see others using it and will come to understand how it works. In time you'll be able to incorporate it into your own stories. Once you have mastered it, you will find this a great tool for making a lasting impression on people.

SUBTLE OR BLATANT

In some stories, the hook is subtle. In others, the hook is prominent or blatant. I repeat the hook tactfully when I tell a New Testament story called the "Gentile Dog." The audience doesn't realize I am repeating the concept of "us and them." I give it several times as a statement, once as an illustration, and finally I allow characters to act it out. I use this approach because I feel if I make the repetition too obvious, it will distract from the impact of the plot. Still, I want the theme to go into their memory so I cloak the hook to make it gentler.

Alternatively, the hook can be blatant. I tell a tale called "Dry Fry." In it, I repeat the phrase, "Because around here, *everybody knows Dry Fry!*" It is so deliberate that after the first two times, the audience is repeating it with me.

The best example of a memory hook is one that helped shape the twentieth century. Martin Luther King Jr. repeated it all through a sermon: "I have a dream." Can't you still hear his inflections and emphasis as he repeated that phrase? His repetition of "I have a dream" helped make his presentation memorable, to be sure.

Likewise, in a thirty-minute story about Joseph, I openly repeat the phrase *"Remember Joseph!"* When I tell the story of Jonah, I repeat *"It's not fair!"* over and over. Another good illustration of a hook connected to a sermon is *"It's Friday, but Sunday's coming!"* by Tony Campolo. Once you hear it, you will never forget the hook. Because you remember the hook, you remember the sermon and its theme.

HOOKING ADULTS

I have seen pastors keep children spellbound as they use a memory hook in children's church. Unfortunately, the tool is often missing when they speak to adults. Memory hooks are effective with both children and adults.

The advantage of using a blatant hook is that it will be remembered. I can return to a church several years after telling one of these stories, and people will come and tell me they remember the key phrase.

The disadvantage of using a blatant hook is that it *will* be remembered. If you do a horrible job of telling a story and you use a memory hook, people won't forget it. You can go back years later and people will say to themselves, "He's the one who told that awful story we've laughed about for years."

CRAFTING THE HOOK

Sometimes a memory hook helps people remember the theme. Other times the hook helps people remember the story, which in turn reminds them of the theme. I tell a story to school-teachers called "Buddy." It is about a dog who is "top dog" in his community. Throughout the story, I repeat: "He had a scar on his muzzle, a broken ear, matted-down black fur, and a broken tail that he wagged back and forth." Each time I repeat this, I do it slowly and with full facial expressions. It has nothing to do with the theme, but because of it, teachers will remember the story. That is all I need in this case, because the story does its job without any extra help.

Most of the stories I tell to children use a singing memory hook. I'm sure those jingles have annoyed parents for days after story time. These are not musical masterpieces but simple, repeating phrases put to music. I will give more ideas about using a repeating song in step thirteen.

Each time we repeat a memory hook in a story, it must be with a straight face as if it were the first time. Sometimes it is light and fun and makes people smile. Other times it is serious, and the repeating phrase is like a bell that holds the listener's attention.

A good memory hook needs to fit the story. It is not enough to repeat a phrase. It should do one of the following:

- Relate to a quality trait of the main character
- Reinforce the underlying plot
- Emphasize the theme

time to practice

* As you approach "Noah and the Birds" and your selected story, decide what kind of memory hook would work best. Should it be a repeating phrase, song, concept, or attitude? Is it more appropriate to incorporate a tactful hook or use a more blatant one? Try to write out a possible memory hook before moving on to the next step.

STEP 7:
Telling a Story Within a Story

Generally, telling a story within a story is a more advanced storytelling technique. Yet, if you learn to use this tool, it will increase your ability to use storytelling as a ministry tool.

A couple of years ago I found myself in the presence of a master storyteller who wove a tale about his boyhood. He told about his childhood town and the unique people who lived there.

His story centered on an older couple who owned a one-room family grocery store down the street from where he lived. Into this setting, he wove at least three different story lines.

His story got me to thinking about a story I could weave in the same way. I might key off his original setting and then say, "What impressed me most was a small photo they kept on the counter. It proudly boasted the images of their seven grandchildren. The photo was positioned so anyone who came into the store would see it, which encouraged comments about how beautiful the children were." [Without hesitating, I would then delve smoothly into a second story.]

"One of those children was Andrew, who grew up and went off to Tahiti as a photographer. During his expedition, he met a lady who was an American, but she had lived on the island since she was born. They fell in love and were married. When the store owners attended the wedding, they were amazed to find the bride's father was an old high school friend who had moved to Tahiti twenty-five years earlier." [This could begin a third story, integrated into the other two.]

Even with two stories being added to the original one, it should flow so easily that the audience won't realize what we are doing. In the end, all three stories would close smoothly at about the same time.

PROCEED WITH CAUTION

This technique is not often appropriate. Most stories don't need it. Still, there comes a time when this ability is useful.

To do this:

- There must be a relationship between the stories.
- Both stories must relate to the theme.
- One story must illustrate a point within the other story.

POSSIBLE USES

To layer stories in this way, I have used short fables, old television advertisements, personal experiences, childhood memories, Bible illustrations, object lessons, audience involvement, songs, and short folktales. The options are endless.

One more caution is in order: watch your time limits. It is always better to stay within your allotted time frame even if it means reducing your options.

---

time to practice

* Before you move on, tell one of your two stories to at least one other person.

---

*

You might have only one opportunity to influence an individual or a group.

*

Chapter Five

✳

KNOWING WHEN TO RAMBLE

> *Memorize your first lines and your last lines, and ramble in between.*

For our purposes, *to ramble* means to tell a freestyle story that conforms to the audience. This enables the storyteller to be conscious of how each group is different. Is the story being told to teenagers in a youth group, senior citizens in a retirement home, children in a library, or adults in a parent/teacher meeting? You can modify the rambling freestyle story to meet the needs of an audience and still keep the story within a designated time frame.

However, there are two parts of a story where the storyteller should *not* ramble: **the first few sentences** and **the last few sentences.** These should occupy a huge amount of preparation time and eventually be memorized. Before you stand before an audience, know exactly what your first and last words will be.

THE FEW SECONDS OF ATTENTION

A phenomenon happens when you step in front of a group of listeners. Few recognize it and use it to their fullest advantage. When you step up, you have the group's full, undivided attention for a few seconds. They give this to you because you are the main activity in the room, and your movement is the most exciting thing happening at that moment. You have their full attention for a few seconds, but no more. In that length of time, the audience will subconsciously make a snap judgment about how pleased they are that you are there. If you don't seize this moment, their minds will conclude they have more important things to think about.

If you lose their attention, you can regain it, but it may take up to one-fourth of the story. It is far better to seize that attention while it is being offered and not relinquish it. In those beginning seconds, know exactly what you are going to say and say it.

Mastering your first few sentences and your closing words are two ways to begin polishing your story for maximum audience impact. Let's start at the beginning.

SMOOTH AND NATURAL

The purpose of an introduction is to draw the attention of the audience to the story, not to your fantastic beginning.

An introduction is like a frame for a piece of art. When you walk up to a famous painting, your attention should *not* be drawn to the beautiful frame. The frame is there to cause your eyes to focus on the painting; unless this occurs, someone has made a mistake.

The introduction and conclusion make up the frame that holds the story. Your goal is for the people to become lost in their imagination and see the events of the story as if they were watching a video. To make this happen you'll likely want to write your first few lines, memorize them, and practice giving them until they are smooth and natural.

STEP 8:
Plan Your First Words

As soon as Martha was introduced, she stepped onto the platform and said,

> I'm so glad to be here today. I have looked forward to coming for such a long time. As Bev said, my name is Martha, and I am excited about the story that I am going to tell you. I first heard it when [five minutes of rambling about Grandpa]. Well, let's see. It's time to tell the story. Many years ago there lived…Oh, you need to know that this takes place in Bulgaria. Anyway, many years ago…

This is *not* the way to begin a story presentation, or any presentation. You need to know exactly what you are going to say when you first open your mouth. You also need to know precisely how the story begins. Don't leave it to chance. This is not the time to "wing it." You can ramble later.

Generally speaking, here are some things **not** to say.

- The name of my story is…
- Once upon a time…
- I heard this story years ago when…
- I am so glad to be with you today…
- Now, boys and girls, this story…

Rather, here are a few examples of ways I start some of my favorite stories.

- "Did you know Jesus took a vacation?" —GENTILE DOG
- "There was a time when I would have made sure you knew who I was."
  —SAUL OF TARSUS
- "Buddy was top dog. When he walked down the street, all the other dogs just moved out of the way." —BUDDY
- "Hiram was a proper Jewish man. He lived in the early 1900s in a little village in what today is called the Czech Republic." —HIRAM & REBECCA
- "Every day, she climbed the stairs and walked down the long hallway. At the end of the hall, she would sit on the little seat next to the window.…There, she would sit and sadly look over the wall that was behind their house." —RAPUNZEL

GET THE AUDIENCE INVOLVED

Several skills mark good storytellers as professional. One is the ability to pull the audience into the heart of the story within the first few sentences.

Of course, there are exceptions that must be recognized. For instance, if I have a classic story written by another author and I am telling it before a group of professional storytellers, I will start by saying, "The name of my story is…It was written by…" Still, even during these times of exception, every word should be carefully planned.

FIRST WORDS AFTER A CANTATA

Several years ago when I was new to our church, I joined the choir. Ken Barth, our director, did a masterful job of organizing a cantata that Christmas. Not only did he adequately prepare us, but his skill in presentation was superb. The audience was moved by the message they heard in the music.

When we had sung the last note, and the orchestra's last chord faded, Pastor Wingate rose and moved up the steps toward the pulpit. I thought, *Oh no, he is going to ruin it.*

Many pastors do not give proper consideration to what their first words should be after a moving presentation of the gospel in song. Usually it sounds something like: "My, what a wonderful cantata. Thank you, choir, for an excellent job. Let's give them a big round of applause. Now take out your Bibles, and turn to the book of Romans." Audience members remain in their seats, but their minds leave through the back door.

As this pastor walked toward the pulpit, his hand made a slight move towards his lapel microphone, giving the sound crew a signal to power up his microphone. Halfway across the platform, he started talking. His first words formed the beginning of a story. Instantly, the congregation was captivated. When he reached the pulpit, he continued the story, skillfully incorporating the Scripture. Everything that needed to be said went into his story. With ease he brought it to a conclusion and gave an invitation to answer God's call.

I stood in awe. I had never seen the conclusion of a powerful cantata handled so brilliantly. The focus of the evening never left the message. I am sure godly decisions were made that night, and it was because "the frame" did not distract from "the painting."

Like this thoughtful, prepared pastor, you have developed your sample stories to a point where you can now add the polish of a well-framed introduction. This would be a great time to practice.

---

time to practice

* Think about each of your two stories, and write the exact words you want to say when you begin each one. "Noah and the Birds," for example, might open with:

  He walks to the window and looks out over the wide expanse of water. He asks, "When will this devastation end? Is there dry ground out there? What kind of world awaits me and my family?"

* Think of words that fit your personality as well as your prospective audience.

A Group Exercise

* Divide into groups of three and have each group select a leader.

* Give a sheet of paper to each person.

* Together they are to brainstorm about the first lines of each person's selected story.

* Once everyone in the group has a story beginning, have each person write it on a three-by-five card.

* Ask each group leader to read one card to the class.

* The class can tell what they like about what they hear and offer suggestions as to how it could be improved.

STEP 9:
Know How It Ends

Susan is telling a wonderful story when she realizes she doesn't know how to end it. In an attempt to solve this problem, she just keeps talking, hoping the perfect conclusion will suddenly present itself. Finally, realizing she is prolonging the inevitable, she stumbles to an end and the story crashes. This ruins the effect that she created for her listeners. She smiles awkwardly and leaves the stage while the audience applauds politely.

You may find ending a story awkward. Throughout a story, you may be caught up in your own imagination, which serves you well. Then you approach the point where you have to gently bring your audience back to the real world. If you don't have it well thought out, you can leave your listeners disappointed.

Another problem is just as distressing. What is the best way to let people know the story is complete and you are about to stop talking? You can solve both of these problems with the same set of actions. Write the exact words you are going to say, and plan exactly how you are going to say them.

I will deal with each of these separately.

SCRIPT THE EXACT WORDS

The following are some ways *not* to end a story. There are always exceptions, but try to make your conclusion more creative than:

- …and they lived happily ever after.
- …and that is the story of…
- …the end.
- …and that is the end of my story.
- …and so, I guess I have nothing more to say.

Here are a few ways I end stories.

- "And every time I read this story or tell it, I am personally moved, because it teaches me…how I…as a Gentile,…am to approach the God of Jacob… Isaac…and Abraham." —THE GENTILE DOG

- "Lord,…Lord,…What…What would you have me to do?" —SAUL OF TARSUS

- "…and he ate both pieces of meat, wagging his broken tail." —BUDDY (VERSION ONE)

- "If you don't know how Buddy got that second piece of meat, then maybe you understand why a fifth grade teacher didn't know how her student, who had so many learning problems, could write this story." —BUDDY (VERSION TWO)

I may ramble in all different directions throughout the middle of these stories, but I always come back to the preplanned ending.

PLAN HOW TO SAY THEM

Ending a story involves more than words. You also should preplan how you will say them. I do the following as I approach the end of a story: I drop my voice a little, slow my pace, and say each word distinctly. After the last word, I stand quietly for a few seconds, take a small step back, and bow my head slightly.

Every storyteller does it differently. My ending is simple and nonflamboyant. Yet it is definite, creates a mood, and does not detract from the message. If I am telling stories to an older audience, I am careful to keep the volume at a level where they can still hear.

time to practice

＊ This is a simple, fun exercise. Listen to various professional storytellers and observe how they end their stories. After watching several, create your own style of ending that is comfortable for you. An easy way to listen to professional storytellers is to check with your library and see if they have cassettes, DVDs, videos, or CDs of various storytellers.

CREATING A MOOD

Making a story unforgettable requires that you create a mood that will stay with the audience after you have finished. The mood of a story is created by pauses, vocal inflections, body language, and all of the other variables we'll consider later in the book. A good ending protects and enhances the mood; a bad ending can definitely destroy it.

Having a definite, preplanned ending helps the teller shorten or lengthen the middle to fit the occasion and time restraints. Many poor stories would have been excellent had they been told in half the time. Going on and on about something does not require a particular talent, but a professional will stay within a time limit.

WATCHING FOR AUDIENCE CUES

The mission of Christian storytellers is to minister to people and meet their needs. If you are not careful, a story can become so personal that you ignore the interest level of the audience. It is a common occurrence for someone to take the stage and use the entire time telling something precious only to themselves.

Many times I have gotten caught up with wonderful memories of an event; I didn't want to leave anything out. Only in my imagination did the audience appreciate all those details. At one event, I had gone over my time limit, telling about my recent trip to the Holy Land. Suddenly, an official of the event reached over and "gonged" a bell. They were prepared for people like me. The bell meant I was to stop my story and get off the stage.

As I walked off, I was embarrassed and perturbed. *That person doesn't realize how interesting my story is. How could she "gong" me like that?* I was upset at the time, but I have laughed about it since. I suppose just about everyone needs to be "gonged" at least once.

Knowing how the story ends gives us great freedom and enables us to concentrate on the attention level of the audience. It allows us to be thinking about ways to make the story more pertinent to the needs of those listening, rather than worrying about how to wrap it up and tie it all together.

A FINAL THOUGHT ABOUT RAMBLING

"Rambling" in the middle of the story can be fun when played as a game, but it also is an effective tool in meeting the needs of your audience. This game will underscore the importance of the beginning and ending in comparison to the rest of the story. Even if you're going through this exercise on your own, you may want to find a friend who will help you through the following exercise.

---

time to practice

* Think through several possibilities of ways you can end each of your two stories. Choose the best one and write it out. At this point, don't tell the entire story but practice its beginning and ending several times. Do this before an audience, if possible.

A Group Exercise

* Divide the class into two groups: the Introduction Group and the Conclusion Group.

* Give each group the following four subjects.
  • Goliath's view of his battle with David
  • Finding a forgotten garden
  • Too many shoes
  • Going to the [city] [country] for the first time

* The Introduction Group is to create a beginning for each story title, and the Conclusion Group is to create an ending for each story. (Big groups can subdivide this task to make it go faster.)

* Take no longer than two minutes per title.

* Put the introductions and the conclusions together according to their titles.

* Have volunteers take a title and tell the story in a rambling style using the beginning and ending created for it.

Both the ending and the beginning are equally important to the story. Both should be prepared and memorized. The last words you speak, and the mood you create with them, have a direct connection to how the story will be remembered. Plan out your first words and your last words. Much of the middle will take care of itself.

The next chapter will teach you how to use scissors and paste. You will need these so you can apply the "finishing touches" to your stories.

＊

Making a story unforgettable requires that you create a mood that will stay with the audience after you have finished.

＊

Chapter Six

✳

THE FINISHING TOUCHES

> *The story intensifies until the crowd is no longer conscious of anything except the events within the story.*

I become a little sensitive about my story when I come to the next steps, because this is the cut-and-paste chapter. I suspect I'm not alone.

Jim labored over his Bible story and took all nine steps to this point. He is sure he doesn't need to "cut and paste." His wife agrees and says he does *such* a good job telling it. His mother is proud and says the story is great just the way it is. He is sure further changes would ruin what he's worked so hard to accomplish.

Then there is Kim. She has put together a personal story that relates an emotional time in her family. She feels it is too precious to "cut and paste." Sam, her husband, is moved to tears whenever he hears her tell it. He assures Kim that changing anything about it would be a mistake. She has asked the local storytelling guild if she can tell it at the upcoming story-telling concert.

Sorry, Jim and Kim. Together we are going to tear into your already super stories. But I assure you, when we're done, you'll be amazed at how much they have improved.

STEP 10:
Research the Facts

Earlier I told you not to worry about studying Bible customs and times. I discouraged you from researching the facts until the time was right. Well, now is the time.

Have you wondered why I asked you to wait until now? Most people feel going to the commentaries and researching the information is the first thing they should do. But, if we wait until now, our research will add depth and reality to our stories. If we investigate the facts too soon, our search may hinder our stories from being relevant to present-day concerns. It is important that the Bible story influence people within our twenty-first-century culture.

Study books provide great facts, but they also provide practical applications that apply to the world in which the author lived. If you read these books too soon, they will dictate how you prepare the story. You will run the risk of having a story that is not meaningful to your generation and the people around you.

After you've taken this step, you'll understand why the storyteller uses commentaries, study books, and input from others provide a profound depth our audiences find fascinating. Recently I have enjoyed reading *The World Jesus Knew* by Anne Punton. There I find plenty of historical and cultural facts that I sprinkle in my Bible stories. To me, it is like salt and pepper for a good meal. You would never serve lunch made up of only salt and pepper, but a sprinkling adds spice and interest.

HIT THE BOOKS

Study books will give you facts about the story that you did not know and provide insights that will enhance your finished product.

If you're telling a Bible story, now is the time to dig out the commentaries, concordances, Bible dictionary, and the biblical times and culture books. (For a list of some of the most useful resources, visit Appendix 3 on page 183 of this manual.)

If you're telling a personal story, this is when you'll talk to others who experienced the event. If you're telling a folk tale, check on customs that were in vogue at the time of the story.

For instance, let's say you're preparing a story on Matthew 17:24–27 about the fish with a coin in its mouth. Peter had been asked if Jesus paid the temple tax. He didn't know how to respond; later Jesus brought up the issue. After giving instruction about the tax, the Lord told Peter to go to the Sea of Galilee and catch a fish. The first fish he caught had a coin in its mouth, which Peter used to pay the tax.

The first thing to do with this story is to prepare it from your viewpoint. Once you come to step ten, pull out the study books. You will be interested in what you find about the tax in question. Then you turn to page 131 in *The New Manners and Customs of Bible Times* by Ralph Gower. You will be surprised to learn that the miracle was not that the fish had a coin in its mouth. Study books explain that the type of fish Peter caught lives only in the Sea of Galilee, and it often has a shiny object in its mouth.

When the female fish lays her eggs, she carries them in her mouth as an incubator. In time, the eggs hatch, and the little fish swim out on their own. The mother suffers from empty nest syndrome, so she goes to the bottom of the lake and picks up a shiny object to carry in her mouth. This can be a piece of metal, a shiny stone, or a coin. The miracle was in the fishing, not the fish. The Lord knew the next catch would be the kind of fish that sometimes has a coin in its mouth. He also knew the coin would be enough to pay the tax for Him and Peter.

This type of information is invaluable and adds greater understanding to the story. Still, it doesn't change the application to your listeners.

PERSONAL STORIES

This principle of waiting until step ten to do research (after you've already decided on themes, determined your starting and ending points, and practiced your story before an audience—even an audience of one) holds true for personal or other nonbiblical stories. Here's why: Let's say you're preparing a personal story about a family vacation you took when you were a child. Your memories are clear about what happened and what the family did. However, every member of the family will recall the trip differently. Their perspectives are influenced by what was happening in their lives at the time.

It is important that you develop your story as you remember it without talking to the others. It is your story, and it should be based upon your recollection of the facts.

Once the story is developed, go to the others for added information; just don't allow them to convince you that your memories are wrong.

time to practice

✳ Now for the homework. Research your two stories. If you are not sure about which study books to use, ask your pastor or visit the Resource section in Appendix 3 of this manual.

STEP 11:
Eliminate Needless Details

You may be happy with how your story has developed since you have started this book, but it is about to get better. These next two steps will change how intently the audience will listen as you tell stories.

It is time to get rid of a lot of words. Step eleven is going to give you the space you need to go on to step twelve. If you are like most storytellers, you are including needless details that can distract your audience. These details clutter the story and may prevent you from taking the time to add needed pauses, facial expressions, or body movements. If your story is to be fifteen minutes long, now is the time to reduce it down to five minutes of essential facts. Step twelve will inflate it back up to the desired length. For a story to be unforgettable, it should be one-third details and two-thirds description. So get the scissors out; it is time to start cutting.

These are the types of details that must go:

ACCURACY DETAILS

We should be careful to keep essential details, but we should never overdo the details. It is more important to add feelings and emotions that make sense to us and our audience.

I heard a friend tell a fascinating story about a dog he had as a child. We laughed until we cried as we listened to his telling of the dog's antics. Later I asked, "Did that really happen all in one week?" He smiled and gave me a sheepish look. "No, John, it happened over three years. But if I had told all the details, no one would have been interested in the story."

He was right. It was immaterial that the dog did those things over three years. We were able to enter into and relate to a little of this man's life. That was the point. Accuracy details would have distracted us from this purpose.

I am not advocating lying, but I am saying your audience does not *need* to know everything. They don't *want* to know everything. It is not important that everyone in the room gets all the particulars straight. This would include: who sat where, what they wore, exactly who said what in what order, what day it was, and the precise sequence of events.

PERSONAL DETAILS

I sat in a service where a missionary told us all the details about his work. Unfortunately, most of what he said meant little to the audience. Soon everyone was wondering why the pastor had given up his pulpit to this man.

Later I was talking to the missionary, and he expressed his despair about the apathy of Americans toward missions. "I spent my whole life on the mission field, and no one seems to care." I wanted to talk to him about his presentation, but he would have rejected my observations as shallow and unbiblical. It would be natural to think, *In days gone by, people would have sat for hours listening to my report.*

A few weeks later I heard Marilyn Laszlo relate stories about her mission work in New Guinea. The congregation listened to every word and understood everything she said. They laughed at certain parts and were moved to tears at others.

Later I learned a businessman, Claude Bowen, had coached Marilyn on how to tell stories. He had helped her eliminate facts that would mean nothing to the audience. He explained that such details get in the way of communicating the story of what is happening in her field of service. She listened carefully, learned the skills of storytelling, and perfected a presentation that is one of the most effective I have heard. Claude has coached many missionaries in the art of storytelling and has been a blessing to many.

EMOTIONAL DETAILS

Before you tell a personal story to a public audience, you need to honestly evaluate your emotional control. This may not be the right time for you to share certain experiences in your lives. If you are not able to control your emotions when telling this type of story, two things may happen.

- You will tend to make your presentation too long, since you will probably not notice the audience growing impatient.

- You will violate public trust. When you lose control of your emotions and the audience is not with you, they feel embarrassed—they don't know how to react.

Don't misunderstand; being personal and showing emotions are good, but only if the audience is prepared. If the speaker breaks down and cries, everyone should be crying with him. He also should have sufficient composure to continue the story.

Still, there are times when you need to vent feelings, and there is a way to do it with storytelling. Contact a small group of people who love you and understand the circumstances. Make sure they would appreciate all the details you are about to share. Before you start, invite them to feel free to interrupt you at any time and express their feelings or ask questions about anything they don't understand.

t i m e   t o   p r a c t i c e

✳ Tell your stories to yourself, and see how much you can shorten them without taking away from the message. What little details can you get rid of? What information is unnecessary? Tell the stories in as short a time as you can. You are going to need the room.

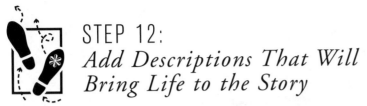

STEP 12:
Add Descriptions That Will Bring Life to the Story

I received an e-mail from a teenager who attended one of my storytelling concerts. He said, "I love the feeling of being inside the story."

The goal of a story is to stimulate the listeners' five senses, to draw them into the story. There should be enough description so the audience will see, hear, taste, smell, and feel everything going on. The old storytelling principle says, "Never state a fact if you can bring that fact to life." This is the difference between giving the essence of an event and being a storyteller.

Description is not factual information. It is feelings and emotions that help the listener enter the world of the story. It is taking an ordinary action statement and expanding it. Description transforms statements of fact into exciting life experiences.

Let me illustrate with the statement "I shot the basket at the free throw line." Let's add description to this action statement.

> I stand here with the ball in my hand. I feel so alone in a room filled with yelling onlookers. I bounce it three times as I always do. The sweat rolls down the back of my neck. We are one point down, and the ending buzzer has sounded.
>
> If I make this basket, our team can still win the championship, and I will be carried off the court in triumph. After that, all new parents in town will name their children after me.
>
> If I miss, a security guard will have to escort me out of the building under the cover of night. Our family will have to move to a different city.
>
> The players of both teams look at me from the two sides of the court, looks of hope, pain, jeers, glares, encouragement, and disdain. I bounce the ball two more times.
>
> I know my girlfriend is watching. If I make this basket, she will love me forever. If I miss, I will never see her again. Bill Jenkins is probably moving in her direction even now, hoping I will miss this shot.

I bounce the ball two more times. The referee glares at me as if to say, "Shoot the stupid ball! My dinner is waiting."

I lift the ball into the air and stretch. The tension of my whole body flows out through my fingertips. With a jerk I let the ball leave my hands….It arches high, moving toward the basket in slow motion.

It's…it's…it's…

I don't know what happens. I faint, right there on the court.

The following exercise is one you will use over and over through your storytelling career. When you apply this technique to a story, you strengthen its character and add depth of meaning.

time to practice

✳ For this exercise, use the phrase "I put on my shoes." Take two full minutes to describe the action of putting on your shoes. If you are unable to keep talking for that long, mark the amount of time you were able to describe the action. Use this as a starting point and challenge yourself to increase it with experience.

A Group Exercise

✳ Ask for six volunteers. Assign each volunteer the task of building a complete story around one of the following phrases.

✳ All six should exaggerate and embellish their assigned phrase.

✳ Each story should be at least two minutes (not longer than three).

- I brushed my teeth.
- She took a nap.
- Frank paid the bills.
- I'm late for dinner.
- Mom washed the clothes.
- I'm ready to eat.

DEEP SILENCE

Speakers often use humor in their presentations to gain reassurance that the audience is paying attention. If people laugh or smile, the speaker knows all is well. Intense description is another way to be reassured of people's attention. It adds a new dimension to how people listen.

Skilled storytellers listen for *deep silence* when they are giving intense description. When you first stand in front of the group, there is a gentle rustling around the room. Once you start your story, the audience will become quiet as they estimate their interest level. As the story intensifies, the crowd is no longer conscious of anything except events within the story. That is when you hear deep silence. Once you hear it, you will never rely on any other form of reassurance.

Learning to be descriptive will enhance your ability to achieve deep silence and thus the power to change lives. People don't make decisions based on facts they hear or even know. They make decisions based on what they have experienced. The purpose of being descriptive is to get people into the story where they will experience the heart of it.

time to practice

* Tell each of your two stories slowly, and embellish every part of them. This is only an exercise, so don't worry about exaggerations. They may or may not remain in your story, but they will forever transform it in your mind.

*

*The goal of a story is to stimulate the listeners' five senses,
to draw them into the story.*

*

Chapter Seven

✳

THE LAST INGREDIENT

> "My critique group
> will come to see how
> well I have listened to
> their advice."

Each of the previous twelve steps is important, but the preparation process eventually requires an audience. Story preparation is perfected in front of people. Our final two steps will require a live audience. Later in the chapter we'll discuss some suggestions on how to enlist a willing audience.

STEP 13:
Include Audience Participation

If a storyteller is able to get members of the audience to participate in the story, it will help keep their attention and bring them into the story. This is especially important with children. The younger the listeners, the more active they should be in telling the story. The better you become at this, the larger the number of children you will be able to keep captivated at one time. Even parents will pay better attention if they know there is a chance their child may be selected to help tell the story.

But audience participation is not limited to children. It is true I sometimes fall flat on my face when I try to pull adults into participating, but a large percentage of the time they are eager to get involved. This requires courage, but it can be rewarding.

Activities vary according to the age of the audience and the personality of the storyteller. The most common is to have listeners say a repeating phrase or sing a repeating tune, but there are other ways as well.

REPEATING SONG

I am not a songwriter, but still my favorite audience participation is a technique using home-made little songs. I think of a few words that fit the story and then sing it. It will take a few tries to make it smooth, but eventually it becomes a song I can use. It is usually a simple phrase like:

Rapunzel, Rapunzel, let down your hair.
Rapunzel, Rapunzel, let down your hair.

I sing this little tune to the children and have them learn it. It breaks up the telling of the story and involves the audience. The children just may remember this old fairy tale the rest of their lives.

Another way to use songs is to create a poem and put it to the tune of an old song. For example, I tell a fun story using the tune from "Shortnin' Bread."

Here are some other tunes that work well:

- Home on the Range
- Red River Valley
- Bicycle Built for Two
- On Top of Old Smokey
- Danny Boy
- Take Me Out to the Ball Game
- Clementine
- Old McDonald
- The Farmer in the Dell
- Row, Row, Row Your Boat
- Pat-A-Cake
- Greensleeves
- Mary Had a Little Lamb
- Three Blind Mice

- Tiptoe Through the Tulips
- How Much Is That Doggie in the Window?

- Get Along Home, Cindy, Cindy

REPEATING PHRASES

A repeating phrase should be simple and recur throughout the story. Sometimes it is best to have the audience practice the phrase near the beginning of the tale. I usually say, "I need your help with this story. When I pause and hold out my hand, you say, 'Go Bill, go. You can do it. You can do it.' Let's try it once." [Audience tries it.] "That was good. Let's try it one more time."

At other times I don't ask the audience to join in. The first two times, I say it slowly and distinctly. The third time, I pause, move my hands towards them, cock my head, say it slowly, and about half of the crowd joins in. The next time, everyone is saying it with me.

HAND MOTIONS

Hand motions are effective and can be used for any age group. Just make sure the audience has ample warning. For instance, if they are to give a single clap at various points in the story, make sure you give them a signal that means "get ready to clap."

Ask the person in charge of the deaf ministry in your church to work with you and teach you a few signs that you can use in your story. You do not need to know the entire language to use a word or phrase. This can be educational and fun for your listeners. And the signs usually coordinate nicely with the phrase they communicate.

USING VOLUNTEERS

I like bringing volunteers to the front to help me illustrate the story. Usually I do this with lighter stories, but I have used it effectively with more serious stories as well. Children will always jump at the chance to come up front, and, if asked carefully, adults will also cooperate. It takes a little courage and a bit of skill, but it can be enjoyable. One caution, however: be sensitive to those who don't want to participate.

YOU'RE LIMITED ONLY BY YOUR CREATIVITY

Another activity would include having one side of the audience repeat a phrase that the other side echoes. If you have objects that illustrate your story, have volunteers hold them for you. When you talk about each object, the designated person holds it up.

Watch other storytellers as they "work the audience." Talk to them and ask advice on how they do what they do. Don't be afraid to try different techniques in front of various groups. It will bring more life to your stories, keep your listeners interested, and you will become more skilled as time goes on.

DON'T FORGET...

That said, though, let me offer three precautions to consider as you prepare to get your audience to participate.

THE ACTIVITY SHOULD FIT THE STORY

Audience participation should never seem like it is something you included just because you read this book. Make sure the activities you use are natural and fit the stories. Make the participation seem so effortless that the listener could not imagine the story without it.

In "Tricky Raccoon," I have some children volunteer to represent the elements of weather and others represent the animals involved. All the other children are singing the repeating song and giving answers to my questions. It may seem chaotic to others, but the activities fit the story and keep everyone's interest at a high pitch.

THE ACTIVITY SHOULD FIT THE AUDIENCE

Make sure the activity fits your audience's age group. For adults to participate, they need to think, *I can imagine myself doing this. It fits the story, it's appropriate, and it will help make the story more complete.* If this is not the case, they will just sit there, and you will be embarrassed. The audience participation in a story I called "Dry Fry" fits the story so well that even the most unresponsive adults in the room will yell out "Everybody knows Dry Fry" at the appropriate time.

It is common for storytellers who specialize in one age group to become skilled at using activities to fit that group. Somewhere down the line, they will be asked to tell a story to a different age group. They should be prepared to switch gears and tell a different kind of story with different audience participation.

A favorite librarian, Vivian Carter, is a wonderful children's storyteller. In our town, people have grown up listening to her tell stories as she led them down paths of imagination.

It always seems strange to me when I see her step in front of adults to tell stories, but she knows where she is and who she is addressing. I know she is more comfortable telling stories to children, but she makes adults feel comfortable when she tells them stories.

THE ARRANGEMENT OF STORIES SHOULD FIT THE AUDIENCE

The way stories are placed in a program will differ according to the age of the audience. Children will sit and listen quietly to any story for a short amount of time. But as time goes on, they will grow bored if activities don't increase. Therefore, save your best participation stories until the end. With children, I start with the least exciting and move toward the most active.

Conversely, if I have several stories to tell adults, I will start with the most active one. This helps them put aside the cares of their daily lives and draws them into the event. The more thought-provoking stories come later in the adult program, once they have concluded they are enjoying themselves.

---

time to practice

* You may be tempted to move on to the next section without doing this exercise. Try to resist that temptation. It is important to get into the mind set of using audience participation.

* I have given you several audience participation ideas. Choose one you feel may fit your story and plan it thoroughly. Then, ask a spouse or friend to help you. Explain what you are doing and ask him/her to participate as you tell him/her the story.

A Group Exercise

✳ Divide the class into four groups.

✳ Assign each group one of the four activities found on pages 76–77.

✳ Each group should work its assigned activity into one of its members' stories and perform it for the class.

STEP 14:
Arrange Practice Audiences

There is only one way to finalize your preparation: tell your story in front of a group of listeners. Storytelling is a form of communication between people. You can practice a story in front of a mirror in an empty room, but communication can only be practiced in front of people.

You already involved someone when you pushed through a story, and you practiced several storytelling techniques before friends. It is only a small step to move on to an audience. I recommend a practice audience. I still use a practice audience to help perfect my stories.

I tell all my new stories at a retirement home in my town. They understand what I am doing, and they are willing to be my practice audience. They know I am not telling them polished stories. They are part of the polish. After I have finished telling my story in progress, a small group stays behind to appraise the story and give me suggestions. I value their input immensely.

By the way, they have become my biggest fans. If I am telling stories to a public audience anywhere in town, my critique group will organize transportation and come to see how well I have listened to their advice.

A partial list of potential practice audiences would include family get-togethers, retirement homes, libraries, schools, day care centers, Sunday school classes, youth groups, campfire and storytelling/coaching groups.

CREATING A COACHING GROUP

The best way to improve your storytelling skills is to create or join a coaching group. This can be comprised of people from the same church, or you can organize storytellers from several churches in your area. There may be a nonchurch storytelling guild in your area that you would be interested in joining. In these groups each storyteller decides how much help he or she wants to receive; the group should honor these wishes.

If you decide to organize your own Christian storytelling guild, the purpose of the group should remain simple: *meet to improve storytelling skills.* The flow of the evening is to tell stories and receive coaching.

If you organize a Christian storytelling guild, we would like to help you let other people know about it. We will put your group's meeting times on our Christian storytelling website, as well as any special events that the Guild will be sponsoring. Go to www.christianstorytelling.com for more information on how you can post your guild and event on the website.

CONTROLLED CRITICISM

It is important to set guidelines that control the amount of criticism given. Here are tips I picked up from Doug Lipman, a nationally known storytelling coach. His website is listed in Appendix 3 of this manual.

Sometimes people simply need to tell a story, and they do not want verbal help.

Others want to hear about what parts of their story were especially good and effective, but they are *not* ready to listen to criticism. Hearing what people appreciated about the story is especially valuable to a storyteller. I have been complimented on parts I was seriously considering eliminating. On the other hand, I have been delighted with a certain section, but no one even mentions it.

Finally, there will be those who are in the final stages of preparing their stories, and they want a full critiquing package, which would include (1) the actual telling, (2) hearing about strong points, and (3) receiving advice on weak areas. If you open yourself to this last area, make sure you do not become defensive about what you hear. Remember, they are only giving you opinions, and you don't have to use them. It is always better to listen now and evaluate the worth later. I may initially disagree with a critique, only to use it later.

CONTROLLED TIME LIMITS

Generally, each person should be allowed ten to twelve minutes in which to tell his story. Exceptions to this rule can be made if arranged in advance. It is not always necessary to hear an entire story for the group to get a sense of how it flows.

Appoint a timekeeper who has the authority to interrupt the teller when the time is up. A little flexibility should be given, especially if it is obvious the story is close to the end. The timekeeper can also tell the storyteller the length of the story, a valuable piece of information.

SHORT INSTRUCTIONAL TIME

Another idea for your monthly meeting is to begin each session with one of the activities suggested in this book. Make sure the group is open to such a divergence from the main focus and that it does not last longer than fifteen minutes.

BUSINESS MEETINGS

There will always be business that the group needs to address. I recommend selecting officers who are in charge of such business, and that they meet at a different time.

ANNUAL STORYTELLING EVENTS

The main purpose of the group is for members to receive help for stories and encourage other storytellers. Still, once the group has worked together for a while, they may want to conduct a storytelling concert. This has the same effect on a storyteller as a recital has on a musician. It also provides the community with a fun event appropriate for the whole family.

Chapter 15 gives details on how to conduct such an event. When you are in the final stages of organizing a Christian storytelling concert, e-mail our website, and ask to have the date posted.

TAKING STOCK

In these six chapters (2–7), I've described the fourteen steps I take to prepare a story. Other professional storytellers use different methods. Eventually you'll develop a process that is effective for you. My prayer is that these suggestions will give you a starting point that will help to equip you to present God's message in such a way that it will have a greater impact.

With the *preparation* process in place, it is time to move on to the *presentation* of the story. We will now turn our attention to some of the basic storytelling tools. You may have developed skills in using most of these tools. If so, I'd encourage you to select the one that represents your greatest weakness and work to improve in that one area.

*

*A good preparation plus a good presentation
equals a greater impact on the lives of people.*

*

SEVEN TOOLS FOR PRESENTING AN UNFORGETTABLE STORY

*

An expert woodworker effortlessly produces masterpieces that will be proudly exhibited in homes. Magazines display the art of professional photographers. Amateurs may work harder at similar tasks, yet produce an inferior product.

How do professionals do it? Somewhere in their past, they dedicated themselves to mastering techniques that make part of the difference. Then, at the time of commitment, they made a major investment in tools and learned how to use them.

If you are serious about storytelling, it is time to put away cheap storytelling tools that cause you to work harder and accomplish less. Here are seven quality tools you will need.

Chapter Eight

✳

YOU HAVE TO SEE IT

With imagination we can see history, the future, concepts, and ideas as if they exist in the present; we can see things that do not exist and experience them as if they were real.

John...John...You're looking out the window again. You're not paying attention." My teacher stood over me with a stern look on her face. It was true; I was looking out the school window but not at the trees. Everyone else in the classroom had missed it, but *I saw it all.*

I saw those pioneer wagons moving through the tall, dry prairie grass. From where I sat, I could see the grass was higher than a man sitting on a horse. It was dangerous this time of year because everything was so dry. The men kept their eyes on the horizon.

Suddenly the entire wagon train heard the cry, "Fire! Fire!" The smell of smoke was heavy in the air. Off in the distance, the prairie was ablaze. With this strong wind, it wouldn't take long for the fire to reach us.

I jumped out of the lead wagon, ready to help. With a sharp eye, I scanned the group and saw everyone else in hopeless panic. It was obvious I had to take charge. I ran downwind and pulled out a book of matches.

Well,…uh…no, we didn't have matches.…That's all right; I didn't need them anyway. I started hitting two rocks together, hoping to produce sparks. If I could get a fire going, I could burn off some grass downwind of the wagons. Then the men could help me turn the wagon train around, and pull it on to the burnt area. If I could just get this fire going, I could save the lives of everyone and I would be a hero. Some of the ladies saw what I was doing, and they didn't understand. They wondered why I was starting a fire when fire was the problem.

Now they came running at me crying in heightened panic. One of them stood over me with a stern look on her face. "John!…John!…You're looking out the window again. You're not paying attention."

In countless replays of scenes like this one, my imagination got me in trouble when I was in school. Now, though, I use it as a tool to affect lives for God. We were all created with an ability to picture things in our minds. We can see history, the future, concepts, and ideas as if they exist in the present. In our minds, we can see things that do not exist and experience them as if they were real.

TOOL ONE:
Imagination

Creativity is part of God's divine nature, and He has given it to us as a gift. Like so many of God's gifts, creativity is often neglected or wrongfully used. Originally, imagination was created for good, but when mankind fell into sin, it became corrupt and began to be used for evil. Even if they don't use it for sinful purposes, many Christians allow their imaginations to lie dormant and remain underdeveloped. This chapter will help you develop this gift from God by using your creativity and imagination to communicate the truth of His love.

Imagination is the first storytelling tool. To properly tell a story, you must see it in your mind. Don't let it discourage you that the imaginations of some are more developed than that of others. Think of it as a foreign language. Others may learn to speak it more quickly than you do, but with patience and practice you can also master it. According to 2 Corinthians 10:12, it's not wise to compare ourselves with each other. God made each of us unique, and He develops us individually.

The more you are able to use this tool, the less you will feel the need to memorize your stories. Imagination is so basic that I am going to give several exercises that will help you develop your ability to use it. I obtained most of these from a good friend, Brian (Fox) Ellis, a professional storyteller in Peoria, Illinois.

IMAGINE IT, SHAPE IT, USE IT

This exercise will help you express your imagination so that others can see what you see.

time to practice

* Pick up an imaginary blob from an imaginary table in front of you. Once you have it, don't let it disappear until you place it on the table again.

* Using the imaginary blob, form the following items. As you do, first imagine each item, then carefully shape it. After it is shaped, use it in its most common way.

  • a fishing pole
  • a violin
  • an apple

  • a toothbrush
  • a cup of coffee or tea
  • an object of your own choosing

A Group Exercise

✳ For larger groups, divide the class into groups of six.

✳ Each person within the group is to think of an item.

✳ Pass the imaginary blob to the first person, who will shape it, and use it in the most common way.

✳ Once someone has guessed what it is, pass the blob to the next person.

For the next few days observe your hands and your actions as you do common everyday activities. When no one is watching, reenact the movements with nothing in your hands.

Years ago I was speaking in a church service. In the sermon, I used the illustration of a man taking an umbrella and putting it up to protect himself from the rain. After the service, a lady commented that when I was finished with the illustration, I released the tension on the imaginary umbrella and put it away. I was unaware of doing this. In my mind I saw the umbrella and used it as if it were really there. Since I had never seen an umbrella vanish into thin air, I took it down and put it away when I was finished with it.

When you see imaginary things, others will see them also. Of course, they will see them differently, but that doesn't matter. When you express your imagination to others, it is like planting seeds in their minds. Your imaginative presentation helps the seeds to grow.

---

t i m e   t o   p r a c t i c e

* Choose a simple everyday happening and make a wordless story out of it. Produce the story slowly so you can think out every action. Remember, if you pick something up, make sure you put it back down; don't allow anything to disappear into thin air.

* Here is a short list to get you started. It is important that you choose something you commonly do.

  • brushing your teeth   • mowing the lawn
  • combing your hair   • putting on your clothes
  • driving a car   • making a sandwich

WORDLESS STORIES

Many people make the mistake of holding something in their hands but not allowing enough room between their fingers for the object to be there.

Similarly, don't rush the action. If you are brushing your teeth, combing your hair, turning a wheel, or putting on a piece of clothing, make sure you allow the time that it takes. Think of how the rest of your body reacts when you do the activity. For instance, do you wiggle your toes when you put on your socks? If so, don't forget to do the same when you put on your imaginary socks.

Once you have practiced, do it in front of some friends and ask for suggestions. What would make the activity more realistic? Ask them to pantomime something for you. Think of ways they could improve.

Few presentations require a great amount of direct pantomiming. Still, without thinking you will reach out a hand and pick up an imaginary object, or brush aside something in your character's way, or reach for something on a shelf. When you do, your audience will notice how real it looks. Subconsciously, they will evaluate to see if you are talking about a story or if you are inside it. If you are not in there, they will not feel safe to venture in themselves.

This next exercise requires the help of a friend whose house you have not been in. I will refer to this friend as Bill.

---
t i m e   t o   p r a c t i c e

 * Pretend you are standing at the front door of Bill's house. Ask him to give you instructions so you can go from the front door, through the house, and to the master bedroom. Once you are there, have Bill tell you how to get to the dresser. In your mind, get an object from the dresser and bring it back to the front door. Don't ask for details about the inside of the house, but envision what it looks like.

Once you have envisioned this trip through his home, describe to Bill what the inside of his house looks like. He should sit quietly during this time and not correct you. Use the following questions as a guide for your description. If in your imagination you didn't see one part, pause, envision it, and then answer the questions.

• What color was the front door?
• Describe any sounds you heard when you walked inside.
• What kind of floors did you see as you walked though the house?
• Describe the various wall colors.
• What smells did you notice?
• Describe the window coverings.
• Describe the pictures on the wall.
• How neat was the house?
• Did you see any toys? If so, describe them.
• If there were stairs in the house, describe them.
• What was the bedspread like?
• Was the bed made?
• Describe the bedroom floor, walls, and window coverings.
• Are there any smells or sounds in the bedroom?
• Describe the dresser.
• Describe what else you noticed about the house.

Now Bill can tell you how correct you were in your description. In reality, it doesn't matter. The exercise is only to force you to describe what you saw when Bill gave you the instructions.

A Group Exercise

✳ Divide the class into groups of three.

✳ Person 1 gives instructions on how to go through his/her house.

✳ Person 2 envisions it.

✳ Person 3 asks 2 the above questions.

✳ The exercise also can be done using a person's place of employment.

TELL ME MORE ABOUT...

This next exercise requires a group setting, and the class must be active and ready to participate.

A Group Exercise

✳ A volunteer tells a small story to the class.

✳ Once the class hears the story, several listeners say: "Tell me more about [some part of the story]" (e.g., "Tell me more about the man—what did he look like?" "Tell me more about the tree they sat under." "Tell me more about why they chose the red ball rather than the blue one.").

✳ The teller should not act surprised with any question. He should act as if to say, "Oh, didn't I tell you that? I meant to."

✳ The key of the exercise is for the teller to make up more of the story as he goes along (e.g., "Well, they almost took the blue ball, but Sam remembered what an old man told him years before, 'If it is a choice between blue and red, always take red.' Sam knew right then which ball was the right one.").

Recently I was conducting this kind of group activity and the audience was full of questions. I answered each with confidence and conviction, which encouraged more questions. It was as if the group felt I had left so much out of the story that they wanted to know. Finally one lady asked, "Are you making this up as you go along?"

I smiled and said, "Sure, the more you ask, the more I make up."

She replied, "I was believing every word."

Strangely, this revelation did not slow down the questions. Everyone wanted to know more of the story.

✳

For the next few days observe your hands and your actions as you do common everyday activities. When no one is watching, reenact the movements with nothing in your hands.

✳

Chapter Nine

✳

COMMITTING YOUR BODY

> *The audience is listening to what you say and comparing it with what they see.*

The Awana leader tried everything he could do to quiet the roomful of children. The storyteller stood along the outer wall and watched the leader's futile attempts at calming the children. He muttered, "What have I gotten myself into?"

The leader looked relieved at the opportunity to let someone else entertain the children. The storyteller took off his glasses, put them in a safe place, and moved to the front of a group of distracted children. He was careful not to allow concern to register on his face.

He immediately began his story. Initially the children only glanced at him out of curiosity, but when they did, they grew quiet. There on the storyteller's face they saw the story come alive. The children watched as the plot unfolded with the moving of eyebrows, the changing of wrinkles on the forehead, the flashing of eyes. One moment they saw glee, the next an expression of fear. They watched his face register anger, happiness, sorrow, grief, suspicion, weariness, surprise, relief, shock, and delight. The children's captivated eyes seemed to be glued to his face, worried that if they were to look away they might miss something.

When the stories ended, the children erupted into applause. They had just spent forty minutes listening, watching, and experiencing a living drama. It had been born in the heart of the storyteller's imagination and had traveled to them through his face, hands, and body. It found a home in the hearts of their imaginations, where it would stay for years to come.

As this speaker demonstrates, spoken words make up only 15 to 20 percent of a live storytelling performance. Your greatest storytelling tools are those that people can *see* as the plot unfolds. The more you commit your body to a story, the more effective you will be in communicating the message. I have seen brilliant storytellers who do not move at all when they tell stories, but they have learned to compensate in other ways. Most professional storytellers use the following two body tools extensively.

I'd recommend that you practice the suggested exercises in front of a mirror. They will help you throw your body into your next performance.

TOOL 2:
Facial Expression

My wife has told me for years, "John, take off your glasses when you tell your stories. People need to see your face." She's right. Our faces communicate life and enthusiasm. Think about the people who sit and listen to you. They are looking at your face so they can interpret what you are saying. They need to *see* the story as well as hear it. Words are limited without good facial expressions.

The main purpose of facial expression is to communicate the emotions of the characters. Facial expressions show changing moods that rage inside a story. These are emotions words just can't express. The face conveys inner conflicts and private thoughts. Writers must use pages of material to capture what you can communicate by a simple look.

BE QUIET AND LET YOUR FACE SPEAK

If the face is to do its job, it can't be rushed. In one of my stories, my face shows the main character mustering up false bravery. Suddenly, he has to do a courageous deed. Fear spreads over his face, and he swallows hard. He licks his dry lips in an attempt to moisten a fear-evoked dry mouth. Panic now has a firm hold, but he moves into action anyway. All of this is communicated with facial expressions but only ten words. Those ten words, in fact, occupy a secondary position in the story. Your greatest tools are those that people can *see* as the plot unfolds.

Facial expressions can reduce the number of words by half and still say twice as much. Slow down your spoken words, so your face can tell its part of the story. At times, stop talking. Your face has too much to say to be interrupted by your voice.

Most people worry they may overdo facial expressions. When they move a face muscle ever so slightly, they feel like neon lights are flashing across their face. They think, *There, I did it. Everyone saw that. I hope I didn't look too silly.* In reality, no one saw it.

For people to see it, you must overdo it. Put on facial expressions as an actor puts on stage makeup. If you do, you may feel like you have gone to the extreme and look silly, but more than likely, you are only getting close to having enough facial expression.

DRESS WITH THE FACE IN MIND

When you step in front of an audience, be dressed in a way that does not distract from your face. I am not talking about modesty. That is important, of course, but I am referring to a different issue. Here are several considerations concerning platform dress.

Focal Point: Dress in a way that causes the audience to focus on your face. Make sure your outfit is long enough, high enough, and loose enough. Others may be able to dress the way they want, but you should be professional and dress in a way that causes the listener's eyes to look at your face.

Sleeves: I watched an older storyteller once, and all I could think about was how loose and flabby the skin was on the under side of her upper arms. I watched a man tell a story and my eyes kept going to the tattoos on his arms. The second rule is, cover up anything that would distract eyes from looking at your face.

Hair: I don't have a lot of hair on the top of my head to worry about. Those who do should fix it so it outlines the face and does not detract from it.

Comfortable shoes and clothes: Storytelling requires a lot of movement, so it is important to wear loose, comfortable clothing. The look of pain on your face should be a part of the plot and not because of tight shoes or clothing. There are times when the occasion dictates that you dress formally. To do otherwise would distract from your story. Still, whenever possible, dress in a way that allows freedom of movement.

---

time to practice

* If you are doing the following exercise alone, stand in front of a mirror and tell your story slowly. Exaggerate your facial expression with every emotion. As you watch yourself, don't stop because of your fits of laughter.

A Group Exercise

* Divide the class into groups of four.

* Have each person tell a story while exaggerating facial expressions.

* After each telling, the other three in the group are to say, "I think your best facial expression was when you…"

* Ask the group to give the class a report of the best facial expressions of all four people.

* Have each group select one person to tell a story before the class.

TOOL 3:
Body Movements

Just talking about body communication is enough to make some people nervous. No one likes to be asked to get up in front of others and do things that will make him look foolish. We all have a comfort zone, and we don't like being prodded out of it.

Improving body movements doesn't mean a person has to look silly. Actually, it is just the opposite. The purpose of perfecting gestures and stage movements is to draw the listener's attention away from you and to your message.

You should not ignore what your body is telling people while you are talking. In some cases, your words may be communicating one thing while your body is communicating something different. The audience is listening to what you say and comparing it to what they see. From your body language, they judge your abilities, sincerity, confidence level, likability, and truthfulness. More importantly, they use this measure to gauge the value of your message.

This reminds me of a community concert I was conducting that was sponsored by a local library. I told several stories, and as it happened, all of them were fictional. During an audience participation time, a man asked me if the story I had just told was a true story. I explained all of the stories I was telling that evening were fictional as far as I knew. Several times that evening I was asked the same question. Finally one lady said, "I just can't get over it. You told us that these were fictional stories, but I get 'taken in' every time. I believe every word you say."

People tend to believe what they see instead of what they hear. I told the truth about my presentation, but my gestures, facial expressions, and body movements told the audience these were accounts of literal events. Unfortunately, some speakers tell the truth with their mouths, but their body movements communicate to the audience that what they are saying cannot be trusted.

COMBINING VERBAL AND VISUAL

The purpose of the following exercises is to make your message believable and unforgettable. For this to happen, you must throw your entire body into it.

BETWEEN WAIST AND SHOULDERS

Most gestures should be above your waist and below your shoulders. When you distinctly place them there, it denotes confidence and poise.

Below the waist: Rarely is it appropriate to gesture below the waist. It indicates people who are shifty, and secretive. I call them prison yard gestures. It also communicates to the audience, "I am scared about being up here in front of you; I would rather crawl into a hole and hide than raise my arms any higher." Since this is not what you want to convey, move your hands higher when you gesture.

Above the shoulders: Gestures above the shoulders usually mean excitement, panic, praise, surprise, or worship. Save big, high gestures for these uses. In all other situations keep your hands below the shoulders.

HANDS BY YOUR SIDE

You probably don't want to hear this, but you need to learn to speak with your hands hanging by your side. I can hear the voices coming back at me, almost *en masse,* "But it doesn't feel natural. It's hard. I think it makes me look and feel stupid."

Before the service next Sunday, look around and see what people are doing with their hands. They are in pockets, crossed, on hips, or holding a purse, Bible, music, or each other. In our society, it is almost universal that people do not like the feeling of their hands hanging by their sides. It feels even more awkward when a person stands up in front of people. If they don't have a podium to hold, they will end up gesturing endlessly.

I know it feels awkward, but we still need to learn to stand in front of people and talk with our hands hanging freely by our sides. Then when there is a need to gesture, our hands move up and out to the front. When the gesture is done, the hand goes back down to the side.

Here are a few exercises that may help. Many have used the first to break the habit of nervous hands.

* While you are alone, tell a story without using your hands at all. No, it doesn't count if you put them in your pocket. Throughout the entire story, allow them to hang by your side.

Once you have done this, ask someone to listen to you tell a story with your hands by your side. This will break the habit of nervous hands and will help draw the emphasis to your face.

So, you don't want to do that last idea. Okay, here is another exercise that is a bit milder. I recommend doing both exercises, but this second can be practiced while no one is looking at you, yet it still gives you the sensation of feeling your hands by your side.

* Whenever you are standing in the congregation during a regular church service (or any other meeting), allow your hands to hang by your side. No one is looking at you, and no one is noticing what your hands are doing. While you are doing this, look around and notice that you are the only one with your hands down by your side. It is a simple exercise, but it is effective in helping you with this problem.

NERVOUS GESTURES

We have all watched the preschool department get up and sing their part in the Christmas program. Some wave at parents; others pull their dresses up over their heads; still others stop everything and stare at the audience with their mouths open. They will sway back and forth, twiddle their hair with a finger, call out to parents, cry, twirl their pant legs, or turn to a friend and start talking. We all smile, think it is cute, take pictures, and are thankful we don't have nervous movements anymore.

Don't kid yourself. We all have them no matter how experienced we are. It can be walking back and forth, curling a mustache, repeating a hand gesture, looking at only one person in the audience, keeping hands in pockets, rocking back and forth, or playing with jewelry. I have some, the president of the United States has some, and so do you. It is what makes every speaker different. The key is to recognize they are there and work on them.

It is okay to be nervous while you are onstage. In fact, I recommend it. Chapter 12 will teach you to use nervousness to your advantage. For now, remember that you should never give your nervousness freedom to gesture. Nervous movements do not communicate the right message.

I watched a missionary make a presentation at our church. He used the same short hand gesture throughout his appeal. He didn't seem to know that it soon lost its value and became meaningless. We all stopped listening to him and started noticing his annoying gesture. I am sure that some even started counting how many times he used it during one sermon—ninety-six, ninety-seven, ninety-eight…If he ever needed that gesture to make a point, he wouldn't have it.

I often ask a friend to tell me what I do that is an unconscious motion. This helps me correct nervous gestures. Sometimes I ask this in the middle of a workshop as an illustration of a point I am making. It is surprising how quickly people answer. They were sitting there watching it, maybe even counting how many times I was doing it. Part of correcting a nervous gesture is the knowledge that we have one. And believe me, we all have them.

The opposite of nervous movement is active, aggressive movement. This is equally distracting to an audience.

Now then, let's practice throwing our face, hands, and body into a story in the most polished way possible.

---

t i m e   t o   p r a c t i c e

* Stand in front of a mirror and tell "The Three Bears."

* The only sound you can make is hums. Tell the whole story with facial expressions, body movements, and hums.

* I choose this story because it contains a wide spectrum of body movements. The key is to communicate the story without saying a word.

A Group Exercise

* Divide the class into groups of four.

* Each group will be collectively telling "The Three Bears," but the only sound they can use is hums.

* Go around the group and allow each person thirty seconds to hum her part of the story. Keep going around until the entire story is told.

* Once this is done, do the same activity with the whole class.

IMPERFECTIONS

These tips are not meant to discourage you but rather to help you. Throw yourself into your story. Commit your total body to the process. Practice what you have learned in this chapter and entrust it to the Lord.

Remember, I stutter every time I get up to speak. Those who hear me have come to expect it. In the same way, God can use you and your imperfections.

*

Facial expressions show changing moods that rage inside a story.
These are emotions words just can't express.

*

Chapter Ten

*

TALKING; NOT TALKING

> *Saying words must remain secondary to your first priority, which is to communicate your life and the life of the story.*

Recently I went to a gathering of professional storytellers. We ate a potluck meal and sat around to tell stories. Beth Horner got up and told "The Three Bears," except she did it with a kazoo in her mouth. Instead of words, we heard the loud humming sounds of a kazoo. She had developed this presentation with her colleague Sarah Howard, and it is similar to the exercise I gave you in the last chapter. The story relied on facial expressions, gestures, and body movements. We laughed and laughed, because we understood every kazoo word.

If you compare telling a story to painting a picture, there is so much more on the canvas besides talking. The large stroke paintbrushes are facial expressions and body movements. Speech is the storyteller's small detail paintbrush. With our voices, we add the finer strokes to the canvas. In this chapter we'll focus on control and use of our voices.

TOOL 4:
Your Voice

Once my father saw me hammering a nail with an adjustable wrench. Instantly he knew it was time for another lecture on the proper use of tools. He instructed me that there was a proper tool for every job. I heard it so often I could give the lecture myself, which (of course) I did when I had children of my own.

Likewise the voice is a tool we must develop, train, control, carefully use, and never abuse.

Here are some ways to properly use this tool.

SLOW DOWN

To use the voice to its maximum potential, we must learn to balance it with all the other story-telling tools. Don't allow your voice to dominate the stage. If you quickly talk through a story, your face, gestures, pauses, and body movements will be robbed of their chance to participate.

Often we feel there is too much to verbalize, and too short a time to do it. I often have chosen a story, only to realize I didn't have enough time to do it justice. That leaves only two choices: tell only part of the story or choose a shorter one.

CONTROL THE QUALITY

The fact that your friends can understand you one-on-one doesn't mean you can be understood in front of a crowd. Record one of your public performances and evaluate how clear your words are. A good exercise is to tell your stories at a retirement home. The residents will not be bashful about telling you how well they can hear you.

WORD CHOICE

Nothing, including your choice of words, should stand in the way of the story. It is never right to be vulgar or obscene. While this is a Christian standard, it is also a standard of professional ethics. Those who violate it reduce the number of people who want to hear them.

I tell a few short memorized presentations, which are story-poems. In two of these, the author uses words I do not feel comfortable using. I simply substitute words I can use, and the audience doesn't know the difference.

STRAINING YOUR VOICE

Your voice is an invaluable storytelling tool and is key to your success as a communicator. Therefore, there is never a good excuse for damaging it. You should protect it like a professional violinist protects her instrument. Your voice is more valuable than any individual story, ball game, joke, argument, or sermon point. Violating this principle is like winning an individual battle by sacrificing the war.

I tell a story where I make loud noises that portray several frightened animals. The first time I told it, I knew I had strained my voice. Since I liked the story, I knew I had to find a way to tell it without continuing to strain my voice. For a week I practiced those loud noises, trying to see how loud I could make them without straining. I would drive down the street making sounds like a mountain lion, timber wolf, crow, and cattle rustler. At one stoplight, I looked over at the car next to mine and realized everyone in it was looking at me. I smiled, hoping it would assure them of my sanity. I may have looked silly, but I was able to perfect the sounds with just enough volume without any strain, and I still tell that story today.

CHANGING YOUR VOICE

The first time I heard my friend Gene Gryniewicz tell a story, I was thrilled and thought, *What a great opportunity, to hear a Russian storyteller. I wonder when he immigrated here.* When he finished and sat down, several other tellers told their stories. Soon it was Gene's turn again, and I was ready to hear another story from the "Motherland." To my surprise, this time he was Irish, fresh off the boat. I couldn't believe it. Later I had a chance to talk with him and found out he was an American from Chicago.

Gene works hard at perfecting his accents. Most other storytellers don't work this hard and usually massacre the accent of another country. Unless you are willing to put the effort into it, you should leave accents alone.

I have also heard men who use a high falsetto voice when trying to imitate a woman. This is only humorous and not realistic. Instead, learn to add just a touch of a voice change as you portray different characters, whether it is a woman's or man's voice, old or young, saintly or mean, Irish or Jewish.

---

time to practice

✳ The following exercise is simple but fun; it can be done individually or in a small storytelling group.

✳ Assign each person one of the following characters. Have each give his own interpretation of how that character would sound. Then the group as a whole works on each change of voice that represents each character.

- a cranky old woman: "Get out of my yard!"

- a mean troll: "Who's that crossing my bridge?"

- each of the bears: "Someone's been sitting in my chair!"

- friendly Irish person: "Top of the morning to you."

- a grumpy old man: "Where are my glasses?"

- Goliath: "Am I a dog, that you come to me with sticks?"

WARMING UP

Telling a story is much like singing a song—the voice must be warmed up. Many people get up to speak, and their voices are not prepared for such an exercise. Words crack, throats are cleared, and before long voices are fading. How much easier it would be simply to warm up a little.

The amount of warm-up time depends on how long a person is going to talk. I am not going to warm up for half an hour if I am going to tell only a ten-minute story. Instead, I will warm up for about five or six minutes. When I present one of my six-hour workshops, I will take the time to warm up my voice thoroughly.

For simple occasions, the easiest way to warm up is to gently sing a variety of songs. I usually go back and forth between singing low and high. I start softly, and over time increase the volume. In addition, I do the normal "ha, ha, ha, he, he, he, ho, ho, ho, hu, hu, hu" exercises.

Treat your voice as an expensive, greatly treasured instrument, and it will help you impact the world around you.

TOOL 5:
The Pause

Jack Benny was an early radio personality who came to understand the value of our next tool. Up to his time, people feared dead air. They knew some noise had to be coming over the airwaves to let people know a program was still there. They assumed talking would be the best noise to use.

Jack Benny changed that and became the master of "The Pause." When he pretended to be walking up a sidewalk toward a house, the audience heard him walking; somehow they knew it would take just that long. When he knocked on the door, he waited and hummed a little tune for the amount of time it took for a person to quit what she was doing and get to the door. He gave up precious talking time, but he gained the imaginations of his listeners.

Skillful communication requires the presenter to stop talking regularly. The ability to pause marks a major difference between the professional storyteller and the amateur. It takes a certain amount of confidence and skill to stop talking when standing in front of a crowd of people. Master storytellers reduce their material, reduce their talking, and give more time for silent communication.

Why is "The Pause" so valuable?

IT ENCOURAGES THE PAINTING OF MENTAL PICTURES

Buddy was top dog…[pause—people wonder if the words "top dog" are an expression or a literal dog] *When Buddy walked down the street,* [pause] *all the other dogs just moved out of the way,* [pause] *because they knew Buddy was top dog…*[pause—people don't know what the dog looks like, but that's all right. They will picture him any way they want until I give them more information.]

When telling a story, we want the audience to watch it on their own mental recording devices. They need time to transfer what we say into images. Our actions during the brief pauses help fill out what they are envisioning.

As I move through the story of Buddy, I continue to give people time to picture everything. I could tell a story twice as long in the same amount of time, but the audience would not be able to create the script, cast the actors, produce the film, edit it for accuracy, and enjoy the plot. When I tell a story, I sometimes feel that people will enjoy their version of it but only tolerate mine.

IT ALLOWS TIME TO EMPHASIZE FACIAL EXPRESSIONS

Don't be like Fred, who suddenly remembered he was supposed to be putting pauses into his story. So he quickly added one or two here and there, but at the most unusual places. He would abruptly stop talking and go "dead pan" with no expression.

An important way to learn how to pause naturally is to watch people talk one-on-one. If you saw a transcript of a conversation between friends, it wouldn't make sense at all. Huge chunks of dialogue are communicated by the rolling of eyes, mischievous winks, raised eyebrows, narrowing mouths, wrinkles in a forehead, hand movements, gentle shoves, little laughs, and so on.

As we've already discussed, there is much of a story that words cannot tell. If a storyteller keeps talking, the audience will miss a big portion of the story and will get bored.

---

time to practice

* Your next assignment is to watch others as they talk with you. By their actions, they will teach you how to communicate with your entire body. They only stop talking because their faces and bodies are in action; most natural pauses come in the middle of a statement rather than between sentences.

IT CREATES ANTICIPATION

When I tell stories at libraries, I see mothers bringing their children to the room for story time. The children are nervous about this event, so each parent decides she will walk into the room with them and sit down. Her plan is to wait until the first story starts, then slip out to continue with her errands.

I start the first story, filling it with anticipation pauses. *Mom picks up her purse.* As I continue to weave the story, the room becomes quiet. The eyes of every child start to widen. *Mom sits there, purse in hand, weighing her options.* I slowly sway; my hands frame mental pictures; my face takes on the look of each character; and the story intensifies. Deep silence moves across the room. *Mom puts her purse back on the floor, and she will not leave until they all go home together.* Suspense always adds value to the story and keeps the crowd's attention.

As the last exercise taught us, anticipation pauses are most effective if they come in the middle of the sentence rather than at the end. For example, in "Saul of Tarsus," I say, "I'm not your usual everyday Jew. Oh, no, I am…a Pharisee. And not just your everyday, run-of-the-mill Pharisee either. Nooooo…you see,…I…am a member of……the Sanhedrin."

IT GIVES LIFE TO THE CHARACTERS

When you continue to talk and don't pause, people have to concentrate if they want to stay with you. This keeps the focus on you and words, but it detracts from your story. Eventually, when it becomes too hard, they relax and go into their own imaginations. Unfortunately, sometimes they do it without you. When they stop listening, they eventually become restless.

Sometimes a story without pauses can be interesting and keep the attention of the audience. What it lacks is time for everyone to become lost in the story and grow silent. Within deep silence, the characters have life. In a story with few pauses, characters are just words.

There is magic, beauty, and power in storytelling. By slowing down, pausing, adding face and body to the story, you stimulate imagination and bring life to the characters. Even reluctant listeners are drawn in. They are forced to put aside their thoughts until you are finished.

IT DECREASES THE USE OF FILLER WORDS

When you are compelled to fill every moment with sound, you will find yourself saying, "uh," "well," "so," "kinda," "you know," "you see," "ha, ha," "sorta," or "anyway."

Slowing down helps storytellers think about each word. We start creating a mood, while carefully placing each character in the proper spot. We don't think about the job of eliminating fillers; we simply no longer have room for them.

A Group Exercise

✳ It is time to retell the story you created earlier in this manual. Tell it slowly, and pause often in every sentence. Tell it slower than you would ever tell it publicly. This will seem strange at first, but it will bring you new freedom as you learn to create moods and verbally paint pictures.

✳

To use the voice to its maximum potential,
we must learn to balance it with all the other storytelling tools.

✳

Chapter Eleven

＊

TURNING WEAKNESS INTO STRENGTH

> *God specializes in changing our weaknesses into strengths.*

If you are nervous about public speaking, I pray this chapter will change your attitude about getting on stage. Sometimes people will say to me, "How can you stand there, in front of thousands of people, *openly stuttering,* and still hold their rapt attention?" It was God who led me down the path of public speaking, and I invite you to join me.

I am the "poster child" for those who get nervous and are self-conscious in front of people. This chapter is for people just like I am. God wants to take your fear and weakness and turn it into something that will bring glory to Him. God specializes in that kind of transformation. In reality, nervousness and self-consciousness are not weaknesses at all. They are platform tools of great benefit.

TOOL 6:
Nervousness

"Are you nervous tonight, John?" Jan often asks as we drive toward a big storytelling event.

"Yes," I answer. "I'm nervous, and it's great." It is great because I know I will do a better job once I feel nervousness setting in. Nervousness is not something you should avoid or hate. When I *don't* feel it, then *I really start to get nervous.*

As I wait to go on stage, my stomach tightens; a flutter moves through my body; my breath gets short and my palms sweat. *Why do I do this to myself? I don't need this.* Others look so calm when they get in front of people. It is so natural for them. Obviously, I am not cut out to do this type of thing.

When someone tells you he never gets nervous, it is because he has given nervousness a different name. This is legitimate because he has gained control of it and is using it to his advantage. Even though he calls it something else, be assured he is as nervous as you are.

NERVOUSNESS IS A GIFT

The key is to realize that nervousness is a gift from God, a gift for us to treasure. Why would He give us something He didn't plan for us to use?

NERVOUSNESS PROMPTS US TO PREPARE

God gave me the gift of stuttering. Because I stutter, my nervousness is at a higher level than most people experience. Therefore my preparation level is usually higher than others. Rarely do I step on stage without knowing exactly what is going to happen. I even am prepared for the unforeseen.

All of us have a natural formula that helps us in this area. It starts with our desire for some sort of assurance. If we fail, we don't want to do it on stage. This makes us nervous about an upcoming performance. Nervousness keeps us working on our preparation. We will prepare until it is enough, and then we will prepare some more. Simple formula, but it works. God's gift works in us to the advantage of our listeners.

NERVOUSNESS ACTIVATES OUR SENSES

Before you step on stage, fear tells you that once you are there, your mind will go blank and you will be left standing with your mouth half open and nothing to say. You are sure the astonished audience will start to laugh, as sweat beads up on your forehead.

That is not reality. More commonly, just the opposite happens. As you stand in front of an audience, ideas flood your mind that never come as you are sitting in your chair. Your smile becomes crisp and genuine. Suddenly optimism takes control. You interact with the audience at your highest ability level. Standing in front of people sharpens your talents. Your senses are awake, and your mind is alert. All your preparation is at your fingertips, ready for use.

Believe it or not, all this adrenaline is the reason we sometimes forget memorized lines. We practice those lines during quiet times, when we are not distracted by other concerns. We are not accustomed to quoting them with all the added distractions that come with heightened senses.

When I have to learn a memorized story, I will rehearse it in front of small audiences. They know what I am doing and are mentally prepared for the fact that I may forget my lines. I do this so I can associate the story with the adrenaline that comes when standing in front of people.

NERVOUSNESS GIVES US AN EXTRA SURGE OF ENERGY

Zig Ziglar tells of a time when he suffered from a bad knee. He was sure the audience felt sorry for him as he hobbled up to the platform. In his mind, he could hear them making comments about how "poor Zig is starting to show his age." That all changed once he was into his motivational speech. He walked effortlessly across the stage; he knelt down as he usually does, and even hopped off the stage and back on. He was having a great time, and his energy was at its highest point. He finished his hour-long talk and stepped down from the platform. Suddenly, all the pain came back into his body, and then some.

Most speakers will testify to the fact that there were times when they were in no shape to step up on stage. They suffered from headaches, sore muscles, pain, sickness, and yes, stuttering. But as soon as they started their speech or story, all was forgotten until they walked off stage.

Nervousness is a gift from God that will help you minister to people even when you are physically weak. It will help you prepare, make your mind alert, and give you energy.

I'm sure the question comes back, "But sometimes nervousness disables me. How do I take control of it before this happens?"

WAYS TO "USE" NERVOUSNESS

Nervousness is a blessing to be accepted and used for good. Denying its existence is not a way to control it, and simply wishing it away doesn't work. Some can mentally put themselves in a state where they "rise above it." Yes, this can be done, but then they lose most of the benefits. Here are some ways that God meant it to be used.

THANK GOD FOR IT

Once you realize you are nervous, smile, accept it, and thank God for it. In this way, you are focusing your attention on who gave nervousness to you and what it is going to do for you. This focus moves you away from how nervousness makes you feel.

Instead of thinking about those who seem so confident, think about those who are not willing to step out of the crowd and go to the front. Public speaking is the number one fear in the world. Dying is the third fear. People would rather die than speak in front of a crowd. God means for you to do a good job, so He gave you the gift of nervousness.

BE SOLID WITH THE PLATFORM

Don't let nervousness walk around. Feel the platform beneath you and be solid with it. Feel how comfortable it is to stand there and look around. Walking may be a part of your story and that's all right. You can choose to walk; just don't let nervousness make the choice for you.

There is another reason to be thinking about the platform. Nervousness wants to move up into your face. If you allow this, you will feel a shortness of breath, and grittiness will settle in around your mouth, nose, and eyes.

Push nervousness down. Think about the stage and how solid it feels beneath your feet. For now, don't focus on your audience, but think about how comfortable it is to be standing there.

BE CONSCIOUS OF YOUR HANDS

As your hands dangle by your side, you will sense how strange they feel. They are complaining to you. They are asking to be drawn up, waved around, allowed to hold something, or at least hide themselves in your pockets. Don't give in to them. If you lose this battle, they will be out of control the whole time you are on stage.

Hands are not free to do what they want to do. They should concentrate on helping you, not looking out for their own comfort. Soon they will participate in the telling of a story. For now they are helping you by focusing your attention down. It will take all your concentration to keep them under control.

MOVE EMOTIONS TO THE MIDDLE

Move your emotions to your middle by breathing deeply and feeling the breath in the lower part of your abdomen. Consciously move all your feelings down. When you make your first gesture, be conscious of your hands being in front of you. Think on anything that draws your attention down away from your face.

DRAW STRENGTH FROM GOD'S STOREHOUSE

Don't fake excitement. False enthusiasm is from the face and not from the depths of the soul. You have the storehouse of God at your disposal. When I know I am not emotionally equipped to stand in front of a crowd, I look to God for help and make a withdrawal from His storehouse. His enthusiasm is real and goes to the depths of the soul. It provides calmness to the spirit and brings nervousness down where it comes under control.

 TOOL 7:
Confidence

When you step in front of your listeners, telling a story is not your first job. There will be plenty of time for that. First, you must attend to the business at hand, which is to relax the audience. For them to get into your story quickly, they have to know they can trust you. When you step up, they are looking for confidence in your eyes, face, gestures, and mannerisms. They are concerned about your ability to keep their interest, and they need a little reassurance before you get too far into your presentation.

There is only one way to put an audience at ease. You must look like you are confident. I am not talking about acting conceited and self-centered. An arrogant spirit comes from personal insecurities and does not communicate confidence to an audience. The audience wants to see you have made an emotional investment in your presentation. If you trust what you are about to do, it starts to put them at ease.

Think of confidence as the sprinkles atop a cupcake. They don't do much to improve the taste, but they make a person want to give the cupcake a try. Window dressing will not help much if you don't have a good story or if you don't present it well. But if your product is good, this will make it even better.

The following are three little sprinkles that will entice the listeners to give your story a try. From there, it is up to you to make it good.

DON'T EXPLAIN THE STORY

I will step up to the microphone, look at the audience, and start.

> Six-year-old Anna looked up and yelled, "Papa's home! Papa's home!" She ran down the lane and jumped into Fernando's arms. Roberto used to do such childish things when he was young. But now that he was eight years old, he was much more reserved. Still, he smiled up at his father, who was carrying little Anna. Together, the three of them walked into the house.

There are a lot of things unanswered by this introduction. That is all right because people are no longer thinking about me. They are interested in the story and want to know more.

There are many situations where you will need to introduce yourself, but when it is time to get into your presentation, let the story make its own introduction.

CONFESSIONS ARE RARELY APPROPRIATE

An apology before a performance is an unrefined way of asking for reassurance. An apology after a performance is a crude way of asking for a compliment. Neither is appropriate, and both are unprofessional.

If your preparation is not adequate, the audience doesn't need to hear about it in advance. If your abilities are not as good as someone else's, that is *not* the listeners' problem. They came to hear a story. You need to get on with it, and leave judgments to them. Save your apologies for when you have personally offended someone.

Prepare as thoroughly as possible, pray for God's help, tell the story to the best of your ability, and leave the results to God. You will cover a lot of deficiencies simply by standing up and starting to tell the story.

PRACTICE USING THE MICROPHONE

Some start their presentation by telling the audience their opinions about the microphone. Others put the microphone aside because they are not comfortable with it. When this happens, at least three-fourths of the audience groan inwardly. Neither of these actions portrays confidence to the audience.

Anyone serious about public speaking needs to consider the microphone an essential piece of equipment. Professional speakers value this modern-day wonder and learn to be comfortable with it. Not every situation requires its use, but you should be prepared when it is needed. Here are two simple suggestions that may help change your attitude towards this necessary tool.

ONE HOUR OF PRACTICE

You may not realize you are only one hour from being comfortable with microphones for the rest of your lives. If you do the following exercise, you will never again be annoyed by having to use one. You may get frustrated by the microphone system you are forced to use but not by the fact that you have to use one.

---

time to practice

✳ Go to the person in charge of the amplification system at your church. Confess that you don't like microphones, but you want to conquer those feelings. Ask if you can practice using the system at church when no one else is in the auditorium.

Once you are there, do every crazy thing you can think of with the microphone. Tell stories, see what sounds you can make, practice different voices. Talk straight into it, and compare that to talking past it from the side. Decide whether you like the microphone in your hand or if you prefer having it on a stand. Compare both of these to a lapel mike.

THE SOUND CHECK

When you are asked to tell a story, find out in advance if you will need a microphone. If you do, go to the location at least thirty minutes in advance of the presentation. No matter who is in the audience at that time, test out the system to eliminate any surprises before you stand before the crowd. Soon you will find out why many professional storytellers take their own equipment with them.

PUTTING IT ALL INTO PRACTICE

Ethel Barrett, who wrote the classic book *Storytelling, It's Easy,* talks about who is to have center stage—the storyteller or the story. This quote from Ethel will help put all we've learned so far into perspective.

> A story, if it is to fulfill its purpose, ruthlessly demands the center of the stage, so its characters can come to life and have their being. You as a storyteller must make a choice.
>
> This, if you have followed all instructions, is not going to be easy to take. Now that you have practiced all the ways and means and know all the tricks—most of them you must forget. At least you must forget them as such. And in time, you will. They will become a part of you, and you will not be

conscious of them as techniques—they are just you, but a newly developed and disciplined you, lifted to a higher plane of artistry. And the day will finally come when you realize that there is not room on the platform for both you and the story; one of you has to go. That will be the day when you forget yourself completely, lose your identity in the story. You are the story. It is the highest form of art.

After I finished the story of "Gregory the Grub" one time, a woman rushed up to me. "I completely forgot you were you!" she cried. "To me you were a grub!"

Oh well. The choice isn't always easy.

*

There is only one way to put an audience at ease:
you must look like you are confident.

*

FOUR PLACES TO GIVE AN UNFORGETTABLE STORY

Dear reader, here is where I leave you.

I am going to hand you over to five people who have written the next four chapters. Each has expertise in his or her area, and I believe you'll appreciate the instruction they have prepared for you.

Chapter Twelve

*

STORYTELLING AND THE FAMILY

written by Mike Mann

Mike Mann

storymann1@msn.com

www.storymann.com

612-724-7074

In 1987 this former baker unplugged the family TV and began reading stories to his children. This led him into telling stories and into a new career as a professional storyteller. Mike Mann now tells stories to over ten thousand people annually. He has worked with the National Institute for Media and the Family to help promote their *Media Wise Kids* program.

He is the president of Northlands Storytelling Network and a partner in Cygnus Storytelling, a cooperative of professional storytellers dedicated to providing innovative, quality storytelling performances, workshops, and publications.

The announcement was greeted with grim silence. Just when we thought it was time to go home to enjoy a bit of the holidays, the boss said there were thousands of holiday cookies yet to be made before anyone could leave.

There was no option, so everyone moved through the all-too-familiar process of preparing for cookie production. There were hundreds of cookie pans to grease, and workbenches had to be cleared and cleaned so pastry canvases could be rolled across the bench and floured. Everything had to be made ready for fresh mounds of cookie dough.

As the flour dust rose in the air, every mind was focused on shattered plans, disappointed families, and the growing distaste for the holidays. Those tensions made the flour dust take on a negative charge, causing it to attach to any available skin and fill every pore. The air became hard to breathe.

Then the rolling pins came out, and the bakers reduced the mounds of cookie dough to smooth flat surfaces ready for cutting. As the rhythmic thump, thump, thump of each baker cutting cookies would begin, Gus would reverse the negative charge in the air by beginning a story. "Did I ever tell you about the marvels of the Sudanese Thygamus Thistle?"

Old hands would exchange knowing glances while newer bakers would look around to get a clue as to how to respond. Although some had heard this story many times, one of us would always say, "Go ahead, Gus, tell us." He would launch into his hilarious tale of a North Dakota farmer who saved his farm and changed the weather in North Dakota during the "Dust Bowl" era of the Great Depression by growing an exotic crop.

The tension in the bakery would start to ease, and suddenly it would be easier to breathe. Gus always saved his best stories for such moments. He never told them the same way twice, but that made it all the more interesting. While his stories were never seriously hindered by fact, there always seemed to be a purpose.

Those stories would get us through the long, busy days and would distract our minds from the tedious parts of the baker's work life. More importantly, they reinforced our values, our humor, and always our sense of continuity. "In this crazy world," Gus would say, "you need to count *on* something and count *for* something."

I worked as a baker for more than twenty years, and Gus was my teacher. Through those years, his stories inspired me to become better at my profession and better as a person. I saw how the entertainment value of his tales distracted us from the drudgery of our work. I recognized how they taught me. Still, I never realized that I could become a storyteller. In my mind, it was a gift Gus had.

Sadly, when Gus retired, Alzheimer's disease shut down his stories and stole that wonderful mind from us.

BLOW UP YOUR TV (JUST KIDDING)

Soon after Gus retired, my wife, our children, and I decided to try life without a TV. Once it was in the closet, we instantly discovered we could do things we had been putting off because of a lack of time. We started looking for other forms of entertainment to fill the time TV had been taking from us. We started reading to our kids regularly.

A professional storyteller came to our church for an afternoon. I was reminded of Gus when I heard her weave her tales. Suddenly I realized I could tell stories, too. I nudged my wife and said, "I can do that."

That night I retold those stories to my children and found it a new experience. I was telling them a story, as opposed to reading it to them. I could look into their faces and watch their reactions. Instantly, I could see if I needed to explain or interpret the story in a way that would help them understand. Eye contact told me if they understood, were excited, or were afraid. We were giving each other the precious gift of undivided attention.

When we give this kind of attention to our children, we are saying, "You are important to me." Storyteller Gail Herman says, "As narrator, you are both connecting yourself to your child and connecting the child to the characters' emotions in the story. You are also linking your child to the values you hold. You are the author and the book" ("Tell Me a Story," December 2001, *Better Homes and Gardens*).

That's exactly what Gus the baker had been doing.

We finally brought our TV out of the closet, because we wanted to help our children learn to deal with it. It is now in the basement and occasionally it does have something to offer. Still, ask yourself, "Is there anything on TV my child can't live without?" Sometimes, you'll find it's time to turn off the TV and turn on your family's imagination.

HOW TO START—YOUR FAVORITE STORIES

I was so excited after my first storytelling experience that the next day I went to the library and asked Molly, the children's librarian, if she could help me find stories I could tell to my children. She reacted with a knowing twinkle in her eye and a dozen suggestions. "Start with your favorite stories."

Well, that wasn't hard. I chose some silly Appalachian folktales, *Epaminondus* and *Soap! Soap! Don't Forget the Soap!* Then I moved to bakery stories: *Bemblemann's Bakery, The Woman Who Flummoxed the Fairies,* and *The Bakers' Dozen.*

You can find versions of these stories in children's picture books, which is a great place to start your family storytelling. Watch out, however, because some picture books are not conducive to a live performance. These writers know little of getting up in front of an audience. The idea would cause them to break out in a cold sweat and run for cover. Many of these are fine books with wonderful stories and are written by gifted writers. They're just not going to work for storytelling. These are literary stories. They will require a lot of adaptation to sound good when told aloud.

Look for picture books written by storytellers. Sometimes the cover of the book will say: "Written by *Storyteller* John Doe." You may have to look in the section titled "About the Author," which would be in the back of the book or on the jacket. If the author is a storyteller, you've got the right book.

Good illustrations of a storyteller's books are the ones written by Robert Munsch. His stories are tried and proven. Robert is a fun storyteller who doesn't use a story for a book until he has told the story to a live audience at least one hundred times.

398.6

Molly pointed me to the books on the library shelf numbered 398.6. This is the section for folk- and fairytales. I found two books that I bought for my own bookshelf at home: *Best Loved Folktales of the World,* edited by Joanna Cole and *Favorite Folktales from Around the World,* edited by Jane Yolen. These books contain hundreds of old stories from the oral tradition. They have been told and changed and adapted for hundreds of years, and they are waiting to be told again. Some may be so old you will want to update parts of them.

A true folklorist would faint at that last suggestion. But understand, this is not a chapter about telling an authentic story in the context and tradition in which it was handed down. This is about telling stories to our families, and the only way to do this wrong is not to do it at all.

SOUND ADVICE

Molly's advice to "start with your favorite stories" was the best counsel I have received. I pass it on to you. Start with your favorite stories and never stop. I tell stories to children every day of my professional career. They often ask, "What is your favorite story?" My answer is always the same. "The story I just told is my favorite one." I tell only stories I like, and you should too. When you are not telling a favorite story, you know it and your audience will know it, too. You should give every story the three Es:

- Emphasis
- Effort
- Enthusiasm

When these three Es are not in your stories: Preschoolers will get up in the middle of the story and look for something else to do with their bodies. Adults will sit politely, but their minds will go look for something else to do. And middle schoolers? They will do both; and sometimes it's not a pretty sight.

LEARNING THE STORY QUICKLY

After I told that first story to my children, I decided to become a "storytelling dad." To accomplish this, I determined to tell a new story every night at the dinner table. In the first two years, I told seven hundred stories. As you can imagine, I had to develop a routine that allowed me to choose and learn a story in about an hour.

I arrived home from the bakery, usually in the early afternoon before my children got home from school. I had enough time to read a few stories and choose one for telling at the dinner table. I read the chosen story three times and tried to memorize a few key details. I trusted the rest of the story would be there when the time came. On the third read-through I would read the story aloud to rehearse the "sound" as well as the words.

My kids loved this special story time, even though I had to improvise when I forgot some details. We found this was a helpful tool to encourage reluctant eaters to "hurry and finish so we can hear the story."

Of course, there was no time to memorize the story. I agree with John; just memorize how you are going to begin the story and how you are going to end it.

THE CIRCLE STORY

Seven hundred stories in two years. I guess my wife is right. I do get carried away. You must understand, I was the main storyteller in the house for those two years. Finally I experienced what I had been dreading. One afternoon, I didn't have time to prepare.

That night I went to the dinner table, and I had not learned a new story. Besides, after seven hundred stories it was getting harder to find a new story I liked. I wasn't sure what to do, but I had learned to trust that God would put the words there when I needed them. So, I just started with, "Once upon a time there were three…" And then I paused, hoping more words would come to me.

There was silence until my daughter said, "…three sisters who didn't like boys but loved birds. Unfortunately, there was only one bird in their whole kingdom."

She then sat back with a satisfied grin and turned toward her brother. He looked at her and then said, "So…uh…they took a trip…to find another bird." There we were, off on an adventure around the table that took us around the world in search of the right bird. Our youngest child added the various chirps for each candidate bird.

Thus began a way for everyone to participate in family storytelling. Instead of me doing all the telling, we started using circle stories more and more. This was easy because over the previous two years, I had given my children the gift of imagination. They had listened to all those stories, so they understood plot structure. They knew what made up a good tale without taking a college course on the subject. With this experienced crew, we created several variations for this "participatory" family telling.

GROUND RULES

It is important to have some ground rules. Telling in a circle can get out of hand sometimes, especially if the kids are feeling rambunctious.

- No one is to "put down" another person's contribution to the story.
- Each teller must help the story along in a smooth way.
- Each teller is limited to two or three sentences at the most.
- If a family member can't think of anything to add, he/she can pass to the next person.

There are ground rules for the parents as well.

- **Be the "story overseer."** Sometimes it is necessary for the parent-teller to participate in the story more often than other family members simply to keep the story moving or maintain some kind of sensible track.

- **Be flexible.** This parent-child alternating is also helpful if the children happen to be tired or lethargic.

- **Don't be too critical.** Allow each child to contribute a different personality and flavor to the final product. Children need to be free to exercise their creative muscles. Teach them to tell their part of the story without being afraid of making mistakes.

- **Be sensitive.** What a child contributes is often a window into what he/she is dealing with that day. How the "problem" in the story gets resolved is everyone's opportunity to offer a solution.

WHERE AND WHEN

I suggest you make storytelling a ritual for your family. Determine to do it, and then set a time when there are no distractions. Our family was fortunate to already have a ritual of eating supper together, so that became our story time. If supper doesn't work for you, choose a time when you are all together.

Several places in the Old Testament, the Lord tells fathers to create "storytelling occasions" for their children (such as Joshua 4:5–7). To apply this principle to our time, we must develop the skill and learn to be flexible.

The participatory method of storytelling can be used in many different places and situations. Here are some circumstances that can easily be turned into "storytelling occasions." (You'll also find these are times when a story really comes in handy.)

IN THE CAR

Storytelling was handy for our family when we took long car trips. It would make the miles fly by, keep the driver awake, teach wonderful lessons, form fantastic memories, and keep the children occupied.

The end of the story didn't always coincide with the end of the trip. Occasionally, some of our stories lasted longer than the trip, requiring that we circle the block a few times while the group brought it to a close.

Of course, if this is a problem, you can choose to take advantage of that age-old tactic of the serial writers: "to be continued." When it's time to go home, this can serve as incentive for little ones who are often slow to put on their coats.

THE DOCTOR'S OFFICE

I remember when our children were preschool age, and it seemed every season had a reason for us to go see the doctor. We spent so much time at the clinic that our kids seemed to be more familiar with the waiting room toys than their own. They would police the other children if they perceived that a favorite waiting room toy was being mistreated. "That's not the way you're supposed to put the Duplo train together. Go back and sit with your mom." Stories helped keep peace in the waiting room and also helped keep the sick child from moving around the room and sharing the bug that brought us there.

AT A RESTAURANT

When our kids were young, our version of fine dining was any restaurant where a person came to our table and took our order. If we had to wait to be seated, I would start a story or announce its theme. Everyone would start thinking about his or her contribution to the story that was to begin when we were seated.

Most of these "family" restaurants used paper place mats, which were particularly handy for writing the story. We did this to avoid disrupting the dining room. Each child, in order, would write a two- or three-sentence contribution for the story and then quietly pass it on to the next contributor. Sometimes the story would extend onto a second or third placemat. With five in the family, we never ran out of mats before the food arrived.

OTHER TIMES AND PLACES

- Stuck in traffic—stories even help the driver ease road rage tensions
- Waiting for the bus
- Any long waiting times
- Long bus trips
- On an airplane—use the written circle story here to avoid bothering others

GETTING A CIRCLE STORY STARTED

Here are some examples of circle story starters. You can use any names you want, even the names of your children.

> Elizabeth, Tommy, and Bobby walked the same way to school every day. This particular day, they decided to go a different way. On the way to school they walked right by a…

> Jimmy did not like to tie his shoes. Everywhere he went his shoelaces would flip-flap and whip-whap around his ankles. He was always tripping himself or tripping others with his shoelaces, until one day he tripped…

> Rena always forgot to pick up her toys. Every day her parents would say, "Rena, pick up your toys." She would say okay, but then forget to do it. Her room got so full of toys that…

FILL IN THE BLANK

This is especially good for younger children or children who are new to circle stories. Simply tell an easy story and have them fill in the blanks every time you stop.

Here is a good example.

> Two kids were walking home from the park one day when they met a big giant
> _____ coming down the road. The children said, "_____," and
> the big giant_____said, "_____. So the children decided
> the big giant_____ needed some help.

You continue to tell the story, improvising as you go and stopping every so often to let the next child in line contribute.

PAINTING MENTAL PICTURES

"When I hear stories, I get to paint the pictures in my head," says Blake, age seven.

A variation on the "fill in the blank" story is to have the children fill in description. Here is an example.

> Two kids were walking home from the park one day when they met a monster that
> looked like_____, with eyes that were_____and colored
> _____, and hair that was_____. The monster had feet that
> _____and hands that_____. It was taller than_____.

Good storytelling allows those in the audience to paint pictures in their minds' eye. It taps into that God-given gift of imagination. Teaching your child to fill in the description for a story adds a new focus on this skill. Educators call it a *visual thinking strategy*—a vital skill necessary for problem solving. Albert Einstein used this skill in the development of his theory of relativity. Jesus used descriptive stories to connect His followers with His teaching.

TAKE THAT!

Here is an idea I picked up from John Walsh. When storytelling is a family tradition, the children will develop the skill as they get older. This would be a good time to introduce the "Take that!" circle story. With this, each person would tell more than one or two sentences.

The parent starts the story and takes the plot to a "cliff hanger." This simply means the main character is in a difficult spot. The next person in the circle must quickly resolve the situation and move the main character toward another "cliff hanger." Once the story makes the complete circle, the parent concludes the tale with a proper ending.

DEVELOPING PERSONAL STORIES

As a "storytelling dad," I was doing fine with stories other people wrote. Then one day my daughter asked, "Dad, don't you have stories about you?" My first thought was, *Nothing interesting has ever happened to me.* I was wrong, and you are wrong, too, if you think that.

Your story and mine are threads in the fabric of the human story. We are the reason Christ came to earth. I am dedicating a large section of this chapter to personal stories, because you need to pass your heritage to your children. They learn a little from what you say, more by what you do, but they learn the most from who you are. They need to know how you derived your value system. Besides, your children will delight in discovering that you were once their size, with the same hopes and dreams they have.

FINDING PERSONAL STORIES

I finally decided to tell the family stories about me. I managed to stumble through personal anecdotes and even expanded a few into full-fledged stories. I found I was not good at personal stories, so I signed up to take a class on the subject from a local storyteller. In this class she shared a "universal technique for developing a personal story."

It is not much different from what you have learned in this book about developing a Bible story, except for one thing. Instead of *pretending* that you were at the scene of the story, *you really were there.*

That's right, you get to interrogate the chief witness. *You.* All of the information you need is stored in your memory. So find a quiet place and answer the following questions. Stories will start to flow from there.

What was your favorite place to play when you were five to nine years old?

There may be more than one, but for now concentrate on one. Try to focus on that place and block out distractions by pretending you are that age again.

What do you look like?

Describe your hair, your clothes, your shoes, your height, etc.

What does the place look like?

Pretend you are standing in that favorite place. Take a look around. What do you see? If it is in a building, start on your right and move slowly around the room. What do you see on the walls? What do you see on the ceiling? What do you see on the floor? If your favorite place is outdoors, then describe what you see when you look around, up, and down.

What are some of the things around you?

Describe them. Include toys, books, pictures, music, etc.

Who are the people there?

Describe them. Include friends, relatives, bullies, teachers, etc. Include pets here, as well.

What do you smell when you are here?

The sense of smell is a powerful tool for evoking memories. Psychologists tell us there are two layers of smell. The primary smells are large and fill the space. Secondary smells are not so obvious, and you have to get closer to notice them.

When I think of **primary smells,** I think of my grandmother's kitchen. She believed that wherever two or more are gathered, there they shall be fed. I remember the smell of turkey in the oven and fresh homemade buns cooling on the counter. I remember the smell of my mother's chocolate chip cookies baking in the oven. Oh my, let's see, where were we?

When I think of **secondary smells,** I think of crayons or the smell of a Tootsie Roll or the smell of Lincoln Logs.

What did you taste when you were there?

You may answer "nothing" to this one, but more than likely there was something. It might not be food because young children put more than food in their mouths.

The questions above have led you through four of the five senses: sight, sound, smell, and taste. Touch does not evoke as many memories, but it too can be a valuable part of your description.

THE EMOTIONS

Once you have engaged the senses, look at the emotions that might be connected to this favorite place. We'll work with these four basic emotions:

- Joy
- Anger
- Sadness
- Fear

Think about these in connection with this place. More than likely, you will think of several stories for each emotion.

I have led many groups of people through this exercise, from third graders to senior citizens. Many find this a good time to take notes. By doing so, you will likely gather more information than you need for a story. All of this extra information can get in the way unless you accept the fact that it is too much for one story. Don't be concerned; this is just the raw material for many stories.

At this point, you are probably saying one of two things:

Wait. I've found a story, and I'm not through all the questions yet.

Congratulations! Continue going through all the questions, using them to flesh out more material for your story.

Hey! I've done all this, and I still don't have a story.

Congratulations. Of the thousands of people who have used this exercise, you are the first one who could not find a story. This in itself would make a good story.

If you sincerely can't think of anything, one of two things may have happened. First, you have thought of a story, but you don't think it is good enough. Or, if you truly have not found a story after going through the questions, there may be a mental block getting in the way. Stop and ask yourself, "Do I have too many other things in my life that are distracting me right now?" If the answer is yes, try to find a way to clear your mind, or choose another time and try again.

If you think you don't have a story, and you are convinced that you are not distracted, it may be time to seek the help of a professional storyteller. They are trained to help you break through such mental blocks.

MY THREE STEPS

You now have the raw material for a great personal story, or even more than one. Quickly take the following three steps at the same time. These steps are easier to undertake if you're working through this book as part of a storytelling group.

IMMEDIATELY TELL YOUR STORY ALOUD.   You may ask, "Why so soon?" We have just spent important time mining precious storytelling gold from your past. If you wait too long, much of the gold will sink back into the bottom of your memory. You must begin now to use it, bend it, and shape it into a story. This is so important that if you can't find someone, simply tell it into a tape recorder or tell it to your cat.

IMMEDIATELY TELL YOUR STORY THREE TIMES.   Why? This forces you to do oral editing. When you go through the questions, you produce a lot of material you will not use with this story. By telling the story, you will become progressively more efficient. This reduces the story to the bare bones. You will hear what parts of the story work, and you will hear what is unnecessary.

IMMEDIATELY TELL YOUR STORY THREE TIMES, BUT FOR ONLY TWO MINUTES EACH. This refines the gold. Oral editing requires bringing the story down to what is precious for this story. Once you have the best information, you can apply the tools and steps you learned earlier to make it interesting.

A Group Exercise

Have each person tell his story three times to three different people with no practicing in between each telling.

* Divide the class into groups of two.

* Allow two minutes for one person to tell a story to the other (using no notes).

* Allow two minutes for the second person to tell a story to the first.

* Redivide the class so everyone has a new partner.

* Allow two minutes each for telling.

* Repeat this process once more.

* Ask volunteers to answer this question for the group: Did you notice how the story gets better with each telling?

ADDING THE POLISH

Once you have told your two-minute story three times, you are able to go back and add some of the details you dropped. Remember to add only details that help the story do what you want it to do.

Becoming a "storytelling dad" was the beginning of a new career for me, but it was also the beginning of being more involved in the lives and memories of my children. Let me change that statement that I heard Gus say so often. "In this crazy world, your *family* needs to count on something and count for something."

*

"When I hear stories, I get to paint the pictures in my head."
—BLAKE, AGE 7

*

Chapter Thirteen

✳

STORYTELLING AND THE CHURCH

written by Margie Reitsma

Margie Reitsma

The Story Connection

www.thestoryconnection.com

mreitsma@rconnect.com

712-737-2472

As a professional storyteller, Margie Reitsma tells stories to children and adults in churches, schools, libraries, and community events throughout the Midwest. Her lively, interactive storytelling connects with listeners as she entertains and educates using multicultural folktales, personal stories, and biblical and historical tales.

Six years ago my daughter asked me to tell a story at her wedding reception. I was honored—and worried. What story should I tell? For months I reflected on Heather's life, remembering stories from her childhood and teenage years. I asked my husband and my other three daughters to tell me their stories about Heather.

We found ourselves reflecting on events from our lives and the life of our family. These stories helped us see God's grace in a new way. In time, I had two notebooks bulging with family memories and possible stories. Unfortunately, when May rolled around, I still did not have the *perfect* story about Heather.

One day I remembered she had always wanted a middle name. After all, most people have one, and she felt that her name was not complete. I mulled over how strange it was that we give our children names when we don't know them yet. I wondered, *Now that I know and love this daughter of mine, what name should I give her as she begins a new life with Dave, her future husband?* Suddenly I thought of one of my favorite Bible stories: the story of David and Abigail found in 1 Samuel 25.

David had been in the Judean wilderness with his little army. While there, he had protected the family and interests of a man named Nabal. This had been profitable for Nabal. There came a time when David needed a few provisions for his men, but Nabal refused to help. David became furious and started to move his army toward Nabal's compound. Abigail, Nabal's wife, heard of the circumstances, quickly gathered provisions, and stood in the road in front of David's approaching army. She pled with him not to seek revenge for Nabal's insults but to wait for the Lord to fight His cause. David turned back his army at the counsel of this wise woman. After Nabal died of natural causes, Abigail became David's wife.

This story helped shape my perception of how a Christian wife and husband help each other in their faith. A wise woman can help her husband (or husband-to-be) do what is right. Both men were wrong, and Abigail stood in the road to stop both of them from going against God's principles. I could see the connection between Abigail and my daughter.

At the reception, I told the people how much the story of Abigail meant to me and carefully told the scriptural account of this courageous woman. When I finished, I turned and told Heather I was finally giving her the middle name she had always wanted: *Abigail.* With that one story, I was symbolically giving my daughter the gift of my love and my hope for her new life.

By the way, that story started a tradition in our family. Each of my daughters has asked me to tell a story at her wedding reception.

LOOKING FOR GOD'S HAND

Although this storytelling took place at a wedding reception, it was more than just a private event for our family. It was told for all the believers who were gathered that night. Our individual stories are part of the public history of God's grace. We are to look at our lives in the light of God's story and view events with the eyes of faith.

Christian storytelling nurtures and strengthens the entire body of believers. Stories affect people differently at various times in their lives. We share the story God has laid on our hearts and let the Spirit of God do the rest.

This has been true through the ages. In the Old Testament God instructs parents to talk to their children about His commandments and deeds (Deuteronomy 6:4–9). If you follow this example, it will be rewarding for your children and for your church family; it also can be a healing experience for you. As you look back over your life, you will recognize God's hand in ways you didn't understand at the time. You and your family will be amazed and blessed by the stories God will send your way.

Susan Schriver, academic dean of New England Bible College, explores the theological role of storytelling, when she says:

> Deuteronomy 6:4–9 is frequently called *The Shema*. It explains the role of the education of children. This instruction takes the form of stories that tell how God has repeatedly delivered His people from the hands of their enemies. These stories express the very essence of the heart of God's relationship with His people and encourages them to remember their journey of faith. Children grasp its simplicity, while adults are moved by the complexities of an intimate relationship with God.
>
> Stories form the fiber of our walk with God. They insure a rich experience for all who draw together to worship and experience the presence of the Almighty.

TELL IT AGAIN

The Bible is the story of God's love for the people of this world. We cannot look at a rainbow without remembering the story of how God promised never to flood the earth again. Every Jewish and Christian child grows up hearing how God parted the Red Sea to lead His people out of slavery.

In the Old Testament, prophets, priests, and kings told the stories. In the New Testament, God sent His Son, who told simple stories such as the lost-and-found sheep, coins, and sons. He took the profound truths of the kingdom of God and put them in simple terms everyone could understand.

Again, allow me to quote Susan Schriver:

> One out of every five adults cannot read....[so] we must move beyond the
> traditional use of reading and writing as our primary means of proclaiming
> the gospel to adults. One of the simplest ways to bridge the literacy gap is to
> reclaim storytelling as an adult instructional method. Here, everyone can
> approach the gospel on equal footing. Much of Scripture is presented in story
> form and can be taught as such without diminishing educational effectiveness.

We all tell stories because we look for meaning and connection in the events around us. An old Hasidic proverb says: "Tell people a fact, and you touch their minds; tell them a story, and you touch their souls."

Stories of faith help us remember God's acts of love in the past and give us hope for the present. They help us remember who God is, who we are, and what God did for us. They become living memorials to God's love. They are His-story.

Luke 17:11–19 tells about ten lepers healed by Jesus. Only one, a Samaritan, returned to thank the Lord. I picture the Samaritan as having a loud booming voice, which made it easier for him to get money and food from people as they walked along the road. When the Lord passed by, the Samaritan could be heard distinctly as the ten lepers called out for mercy. Jesus told them to go and show themselves to the priest. All ten seemed to pass this simple test of faith, because they were healed as they went down the path to do as they were told. Only the loudmouthed Samaritan turned back and ran after Jesus. Falling on his knees, he looked up into the face of the Master and earnestly thanked Him. I like to think the Samaritan used his loud voice from that day on to tell everyone what Jesus had done for him.

Think of churches full of people like the Samaritan, who are so full of praise for God's mercy and love that the stories just burst out of them. These are ordinary believers sharing the stories of God's grace. Some sing the stories, others preach or teach them, and some simply tell them. You may or may not have talents in these other areas, but perhaps you have always been good at telling stories. Consider giving this ability to God and see what He will do with it. Stories of faith will strengthen you as well as those around you.

START A STORYTELLING MINISTRY

Storytelling can bring excitement and new opportunities to every ministry of the church, whether it involves worship, education, fellowship, nurturing, or outreach. Here are some practical ways storytelling can enhance these ministries.

IN THE WORSHIP SERVICE

There are as many opportunities to use stories in a worship service as there are to use music. They can be used:

- to highlight special themes
- to enrich a missions conference
- to give the history of hymns and songs
- to offer thanksgiving for a special blessing
- to fit in with a cantata or special music
- to emphasize a seasonal theme
- to highlight stewardship
- to enhance preaching

All storytelling has three distinct components: the story, the teller, and the audience. In your planning, consider all three. Here are a few issues to consider.

- How long should the story be?
- Is it meant to prepare listeners for the sermon, or is it the sermon?
- Is it meant for children or the entire congregation?
- How formal or informal is the service?
- Who is the best person to present the story?

Most worship service storytelling falls into one of two categories: a story based on a general theme (such as stewardship) or a story from a Bible text. I will deal with each of these separately.

GENERAL THEME STORIES

Telling a story with a general theme allows more flexibility in the type of story to choose. You can select a folktale, parable, personal story, historical tale, or a fable. Folktales embody universal themes and struggles, such as the power of living, compassion, greed, peace, justice, or friendship. If adapted to fit the situation, it is usually appropriate to share these rich stories in a worship service.

When our pastor was giving a series of sermons on the seven deadly sins, he asked me to tell a story about greed. I chose a folktale I had shared two months earlier at a prison church service. It is based on a Hindu parable called "The Ruby" and deals with the true meaning of treasure. You can find a version of this story in the book *More Ready-to-Tell Tales from Around the World*, edited by David Holt and Bill Mooney.

I was uneasy with the idea of telling a Hindu parable in a church service, so I adapted it without destroying the original message. I decided to place the setting in a small town in the United States and change the ruby to a pearl. Instead of a Hindu priest, the main character was a wise man who chose to live a simple life. I also adapted the ending to create a more direct thrust. With all this, I remained true to the original power and beauty of the parable. I told the story before the sermon to prepare people for the message. I have since shared that story in different contexts, including a mission for the homeless.

Often it is necessary to create the right context for the story in the introduction. As John told you earlier, it is critical to plan out every word of your introduction to maximize audience impact.

Imagine you have been asked to share a children's message to fit with the sermon on nurturing each other as believers. You choose the folktale *Stone Soup*. You could introduce it by telling the children, "No! It's mine. He can't have it! Have you ever been asked to give up something of yours to help someone else? Doesn't sound too good, does it? Well, wait until you hear this story." It is important to create a context, but don't point toward a moral until it is time.

BIBLE TEXT STORIES

When telling a specific passage of Scripture during an adult church service, there are two methods you'll find useful. Both strive to remain faithful to the intent of the Scripture passage but portray the story differently.

- **Telling what is written:** The first method is to retell the story as closely as possible to the way it was written in the text. While the goal is to embody the text in story, this method strives for at least 75 percent word accuracy and 90 percent content accuracy. This method results in a powerful oral retelling of the actual words of the passage and is frequently associated with the Network of Biblical Storytellers. Although I admire this method, it is not the one I usually choose.

- **Embellishing the text:** The second method involves adapting the story while remaining true to the meaning of the text. It adds practical everyday life to the characters by emphasizing the story elements: character, action, setting, meaning. Although many of the same words in the text may be used, the focus is not on reproducing exact word accuracy. Instead, the goal is to interpret the text to help people hear the meaning in a fresh, new way.

For example, I was asked to tell a story based on Mark 1:29–39, the passage where Jesus healed Peter's mother-in-law and then healed a crowd of people who were brought to the house. In preparation, I read the passage several times and compared Mark's slant with the other Gospels. I later studied Bible study books for context. I looked for linking phrases, words, and concepts, which often give clues about the focus or theme.

I contrasted the *private* healing of Peter's mother-in-law and the *public* healing that happened afterward. This public and private theme carried over into the next scene as well. There, Jesus went off alone to pray until the disciples came to get Him because of the crowds. In my mind, the two events came together—private healing before public healing, private prayer before public ministry. I decided to make vital prayer the focus of my retelling of the story.

The story preceded the sermon, and I told it in the person of Peter's wife because she would have an overall view of the events. I emphasized that private prayer made it possible for Jesus to minister to others publicly. After finishing the story, I listened to the sermon and was amazed by how closely my presentation complemented the points of the sermon. Instead of drawing attention away from the message, the story accentuated it. Many people commented on how it helped them hear the passage in a new, personal way, which is the heart of storytelling as a ministry.

EDUCATIONAL MINISTRIES

Churches have always used storytelling in their children's ministries. My objective in this section is to show how it can also play a vital role in all educational ministries of the church. The core of the church educational ministry is to learn more about who God is and what it means to be His child. Stories of faith help us remember and understand God's acts of love in the past and give us hope and direction for the future.

ADULT SUNDAY SCHOOL CLASSES AND GROUP DISCUSSIONS

Several years ago, I gave a six-week adult study on Ruth. At the beginning of each class, I told the passage for that day in story form. Most of the people had already read the text, but this retelling of the account made it fresh. We spent the rest of the class discussing questions I had prepared. Having the passage vividly in their minds made discussions lively and interesting. It created excitement for the passage.

TEACHER TRAINING, SEMINARS, RETREATS

Telling stories at these events is always appropriate, and the informal setting is ideal for storytelling activities. Providing a safe, relaxed environment encourages those attending to tell their own stories. Group involvement can increase communication between friends, couples, and fellow believers.

Here is an idea used successfully by David Keesey-Berg, a retired pastor and professional storyteller from Madison, Wisconsin.

> If we can get people to tell stories, it will help them reflect on what has shaped their lives. After all, we are all aching to tell a story. We simply want to know that someone is interested in listening to it.
>
> I use a process I call, "searching for hidden treasures." To get started, I prime the pump by sharing one or two personal stories. Then I ease the group into telling their stories by asking them to share a memory that is easy to talk about. I have them turn to a

partner and tell about a treasured place from their childhood, perhaps a home they lived in before age ten. They are also to tell what made it a treasured place for them.

It is important to train each person to be an intense listener. An attentive listening ear has a powerful impact upon a person who is telling a story. There are three simple instructions:

- Ask questions to draw more of the story out of the teller.
- Don't start telling your own story.
- Be prepared to "retell" the partner's story to the group.

This first session is an enjoyable experience, and each person has fun sharing a story with a partner and retelling the partner's story. In the next session, we ask the group to dig deeper into their memories and think of a treasured person from their early life. They are to tell why this person was so special. Listeners have the same three instructions.

In the last session, we ask people to share a memory about a treasured event. These are experiences that make an individual the kind of person he has become. It should be made clear that a treasured event can be something difficult and painful or happy and positive.

This time the listeners will not be asked to retell their partner's story. Each person has the opportunity to tell her treasured event to the group, but no one will be coerced.

You will find this process a great way to increase communications, improve listening skills, and deepen a person's spiritual walk.

SUMMER CAMP, VACATION BIBLE SCHOOL, AND YOUTH CLUBS

Almost any story can be used effectively in youth camps and clubs. Continuing stories are especially effective in these settings. You could have Missionary John tromping through the jungle when a lion steps out into the path. You become descriptive and tell the needs of the hungry lion and the fears of the defenseless man. "Suddenly the lion lunges towards John and …Oh my, look at the time. We will have to continue this tomorrow."

You can use fun stories to help motivate young people. Humor relaxes people and puts them in the mood to listen. You can share animal fables, group participation stories, folktales, stories of mystery, or funny stories from your life. It is usually best to give several of these in a row and conclude by telling one with a godly message.

When talking to young people, I enjoy telling the Cajun fable *Old Mister Buzzard and Chicken Hawk* (*Cajun Folktales* by J. J. Reneaux). This funny little fable is about a slow-talking buzzard and a know-it-all chicken hawk. It leads to discussions on peer pressure, life values, and knowing God's direction in your life. Once I saw a young man a year after telling this story, and he immediately began talking about *Old Mister Buzzard.*

A MINISTRY OUTREACH

Storytelling can be used for all the ministries within the church, but it is also a wonderful method of reaching out into many areas of the community. It can give your church exposure and afford opportunities to share your values and beliefs.

You can influence children outside your ministry by telling them stories of courage, compassion, and perseverance. From the legend of John Henry to the heroes of September 11, history is full of stories about people who had the courage of their convictions.

We have discussed how personal stories help create connections between believers. With a little research, you can develop stories from history that will catch the interest of the people of your community. These would be accounts of events, people, and experiences that helped shape our nation. Many people in our past lived by godly, biblical principles. Just as Israel was to rehearse their wonderful history, so should we remind our communities of their heritage.

One of my favorite stories to share at service clubs, women's groups, and community events is about pioneer Methodist circuit rider Peter Cartwright (*Tales of that Frontier* by Everett Dick). He was a larger-than-life figure, and I introduce him by saying, "God's grace sometimes surprises us." It's a rollicking, slapstick story; but just at the point where everyone is laughing, it delivers a surprise and points to God's amazing grace. It sets the mood for more serious stories.

I usually include at least one pioneer tale when I tell stories to senior citizens. Occasionally, I use a historical setting as the framework for a tall tale. One evening I was telling a tall tale using the 1936 Iowa blizzard as its backdrop. When I finished, a lady came up and told me she and her husband were married on the day of that storm. After the wedding, they almost got lost in the blizzard. I could see from her expression as she told this to me that she was reliving that day. It amazes me how one story can call up another and build connections.

Think of special holidays as opportunities to share stories in your community (Memorial Day, Thanksgiving, Christmas, Easter, President's Day, etc.). Your local library and senior citizen center may be looking for programs. Consider volunteering to share stories at a school. Intergenerational storytelling benefits both the children and the adults. Hospitals also are glad to have someone come in and read, tell stories, or talk to patients.

Here is a short list to get you started.

- libraries
- town events
- women's clubs
- YMCA/YWCA
- Boy Scouts/Girl Scouts
- RV camps
- hospitals
- Christian concerts
- schools
- community celebrations
- men's groups
- 4H clubs
- service clubs
- state parks
- community parks and recreation

Your stories may connect with someone who has desperate needs, and you may not even know it. There are times when I finish a set of stories and I am sure I have not touched a single life. I will smile the best I can as I receive the usual compliments, knowing people are just being nice. Then one person walks up and thanks me for a particular story; I know by the look on the face that it ministered deep into the soul.

*

The joy of storytelling is receiving more than you give.

Chapter Fourteen

*

STORYTELLING AND EDUCATION

written by Michael Lockett

Dr. Michael Lockett is the director of Title I and summer programs for the Peoria [Illinois] Public Schools and a prominent figure in IASA and Title I activities in Illinois. For three decades he has been a teacher, educational consultant, and professional storyteller. He has told stories and given presentations for more than twelve hundred audiences across the United States, including International Reading Association conferences.

If you asked any of my students what they remembered most, I daresay it would not be the plans or the papers. They would tell you about the stories that brought the lessons to life. The most frequent comment would be, "He told us a story." This often would be followed by, "I remember the story about…"

Storytelling is among the most effective tools in my teacher's repertoire. It can be a story about Mathematical Ralph—the "greater than" and "less than" alligator; or it may be about a character in history or social studies.

My first storytelling mentors were two aging Sunday school teachers: Myrtle and Gunhilde. Before I even entered school, I was on my way to getting the greatest kind of education with

Bible stories told by these two saints. I was thrilled when it came time for them to uncover the sky blue flannel board. They captivated our small army of wiggly pagans and turned them into eager young listeners. Through stories told with love, we became devoted learners of the spoken Word for at least a few minutes each week.

When I grew old enough to attend church with the adults, I returned to the children's classes whenever I was allowed. In time, I became one of the teachers and soon found that students listened when I used stories.

When I became a public school teacher, I reached back into the past and used what worked. Would I have become a storyteller without those Sunday morning lessons? Perhaps, because some of my best teachers in school also used stories in their teaching. Still, it's hard to wear a flannel shirt today without saying thanks to Gunhilde and Myrtle for sharing Bible stories on the flannel board.

OPEN-DOOR STORYTELLING

At first, I told most of my tales with the classroom door shut. I was worried about what others would think if they saw what I was doing to help my students perform at high levels. Then I attended a meeting of the Illinois Reading Council and heard teachers and administrators talking about using storytelling as a legitimate teaching tool. That is when my classroom door opened, and I started telling more stories to my students. It was also the start of my becoming a professional storyteller and speaker for schools, conferences, and churches.

At the beginning of my career, *Children and Books* was required reading for teacher preparation classes. It says, "Children miss a unique experience with literature if they never hear a gifted storyteller." Unfortunately, many educators are still waiting for someone to provide evidence that storytelling works in the classroom. I am convinced that when they finally see the benefits storytelling can provide students, they will become "teaching storytellers" as well.

NO BOOK BETWEEN

When teachers put down the storybook and simply tell the story, they are able to read the eyes of their students and react to their gestures and body language. The setting becomes more intimate, and listeners are not limited by what the author wrote. They are free to envision their own tales in their minds. With storytelling, each listener takes away a different mental image of the story.

I did not eliminate reading aloud to students; nor should you. Certain stories beg to be read aloud. Still, one of the best compliments I ever received was when a student at Oakdale School in Normal, Illinois, looked at me after a program and said, "Mr. Story, those were the best special effects I have ever seen."

MORE SPONTANEITY AND FEELING

It was an ego boost the day I walked into the kindergarten classroom at Glen Oak School in Peoria, Illinois, and saw little faces brighten up. This was my second visit to the class. I said, "You remember what I like to do?" I had to wait a few long seconds for the students to realize it was okay to talk aloud and participate in the discussion.

"You read us stories." I figured this was a perfect time to read a short book aloud and then tell the same story. The intimacy increased when I told it. I sped up the tempo and slowed it down to match the energy level of the class. The students bubbled with excitement when we discussed the difference between reading a story and telling it.

As I told the stories, I made changes on the spot based on the spontaneous behaviors I observed. In one story, *The Squeaky Door,* my telling improved greatly when I made a change, mid-story, based on a student's reaction. When I had Grandma kiss her grandson good night in the story, one young man said, "Yuck! Yuck! Yuck!" and wiped his face with the back of his hand. He made a motion of disgust and threw that kiss away. I immediately copied that spontaneous gesture, making the tale better than ever. You can control the whole spirit and attitude of the class when you read faces and react to student needs.

SETTING THE BAIT

The first question students ask after every storytelling program is, "Where can I get that book?" This is as true of adults as it is of children. When teachers share stories with students, those books disappear from the library at a faster rate than others. Storytelling and reading aloud are both effective at piquing student interest in reading books.

Teachers become creatures of habit throughout their careers. We find a story that becomes our favorite, and we tell it year after year. One of my favorites is *Where the Red Fern Grows,* by Wilson Rawls. Former students would tell incoming students about the sound effects I used as I read it aloud. Some would enter my class already having bought the book. When I saw that, I knew the bait had been taken.

This kind of bait is what caused children and adults to demand that Bill Harley, a renowned storyteller, put his recorded stories in print. Children revel at hearing his predictable stories. Try telling one of Harley's stories to your class, and watch how often the book is checked out.

IMPROVING COMPREHENSION

In my doctoral research, I learned that at-risk students tend to learn best by listening. I found that reading aloud and telling stories to them for at least fifteen minutes a day can help them in reading comprehension, and math.

When young children hear stories, their language skills and comprehension improve. Schools across America are finding that students need more experiences with hearing sounds and connecting them with letters. They need to be taught that the letters form words, words form sentences, sentences form paragraphs, and paragraphs they are trying to read have meaning relevant to the stories they have heard. Storytelling is the perfect bridge that carries students over the gap between instruction in reading skills and true comprehension of text.

Students today are suffering from *word poverty.* John Giles, author of *The First Forest,* quoted research showing that in 1945 the average elementary student knew 45,000 vocabulary words. At the end of the twentieth century, the average elementary student knew 10,000 words. This means today's students know fewer than 25 percent of the vocabulary words their parents and grandparents knew. According to Ruby Payne, the situation is worse for students in generational poverty.

During casual talk among peer groups, students use between 400 and 800 words. Is it any wonder that teachers have difficulty promoting reading? Storytelling and reading aloud to students are good tools to help students improve their vocabularies and reverse this deficit. The more words they hear and understand, the better chance they will recognize them in print.

HEARING LITERATURE

Storytelling teachers introduce children to quality literature that otherwise might be missed. Literature becomes a source of pleasure when the teacher connects books with storytelling.

Reading a favorite book aloud in class develops closeness between teachers and children. Oh, the thrill to watch students' faces as you read *Charlotte's Web,* by E. B. White. They may have seen the movie, or even read the book, but hearing it is a new experience. They sit in rapt attention with eyes wide open. Sharing a tale through storytelling will often point the way to an entire section of literature that may have been overlooked.

IMPROVING WRITING SKILLS

When students become better readers, they also become better writers. Storytelling provides scaffolding on which students can build their own stories in written form. It offers ways to bring children into the act of storymaking. Some suggestions would be to encourage students to create their own endings to stories, keep a story's characters and setting but alter the main problems, or rewrite old stories with a modern spin.

The National Research Council (1999) has encouraged the activity of having young children dictate their stories. With this the teacher says, "You tell me the story, and I'll write the words." After the dictation, the teacher asks questions about the story to fill in the things that are missing.

A simple story often can help the ultimate writing challenge—the student who claims to have "nothing to write about." I tell a version of a Yiddish folktale of the tailor who makes a story out of nothing. Look for a version of the story as told in *Just Enough to Tell a Story,* by Nancy Schimmel (Two Sisters Press).

INSTRUCTION IN READING AND LANGUAGE ARTS

Ways storytelling affects students in the classroom:

- Enhance children's curiosity
- Provides direct instruction in *cause and effect*
- Expands students' creativity
- Improves students' ability to recall information
- As the story progresses, students develop the skill of making predictions
- Students learn sequencing and summarizing along with story mapping

CONTENT AREA INSTRUCTION

I begin to walk around the classroom, talking about a skinny old man who walked through an Indian village one day. "Where you going, Gandhi?" I ask out loud.

Then, answering for Gandhi, I say, "To the sea to get some salt."

The villagers quickly protest, "But that's illegal."

"I know it," says Gandhi.

The people become alarmed. "But you'll be put in jail!"

The old man looks at everyone in the crowd. Slowly and quietly he says, "I know, but the jails can't hold everyone."

At this, I take a student by the hand—encouraging him to join the march to the sea. Suddenly the "I" becomes "we." The class copies the pattern, and more students join the march.

In less than five minutes, the stage is set for talking about how Gandhi's leadership brought India to independence. The few minutes I spend telling a small part of the tale of *Gandhi's Salt March* and acting it out leads students to research the topic. They come back to class excited about sharing more details.

This gives students a basis on which to compare those actions with those of Martin Luther King Jr., who used passive resistance during the fight for civil rights in America. If I want to show how powerful the spoken word can be, I might read aloud the text of the "I Have a Dream" speech, which is a series of mental pictures.

Capturing the interest of the students is my favorite way to use a story. Madeline Hunter calls it "anticipatory set," and it is usually done at the beginning of class. The story catches the attention of every student and helps them focus on the lesson.

I am not saying it is the job of the content area teacher to entertain students. Rather we are to endeavor to create a love for learning in the heart of every student. Teachers should work to develop a collection of stories and interesting facts that relate to their teaching. Inserting the right story at the right moment can have a positive effect on a targeted student or on the entire class.

Additionally, using short anecdotes is an easy way to bring informal storytelling into the classroom. It serves to relieve tension and makes the classroom seem warmer and friendlier.

Consider, for example, a student with a ruined science experiment. This student is not in the best state of mind to benefit from further instruction. What a great opportunity to take a few minutes and relate a tragic experience in the life of Thomas Edison. His entire laboratory in Menlo Park had burned to the ground. Edison would have had every right to be angry and full of self-pity, but instead he said the event was a blessing. "All of my mistakes have now been burned up, and I can start over." Two days later, Edison invented the electric lightbulb.

TIME TO START TELLING

I was hesitant to give workshops and programs for adults at churches. My reasoning was simple. I told stories to children. Even in my youth, I felt comfortable telling stories to children in Sunday school. I knew education, and I loved teaching, but church leaders were a different matter. I wasn't interested in telling stories to them. After all, they knew the Bible, the source of the greatest stories. Still, I felt a calling that gave me misgivings and discomfort.

One Sunday, our pastor talked about Jonah and his reluctance to go to Nineveh. Wow, did I ever identify with that old prophet. I thought about it all week.

The next Saturday, I was driving across town with my wife and decided to discuss the issue with her. I told her I felt I was being called to write stories and materials for churches and Sunday schools, but I didn't want to do it. I confessed this made me feel like Jonah. What I wanted to do was give more programs in schools, speak at educational conferences, and publish stories in that setting. Still, I didn't want to be like Jonah and not follow what God was asking me to do. I definitely didn't want to get swallowed into some sort of "whale's belly." I concluded my little confession with "I wish God would give me a sign."

My wife's encouraging and supportive response was, "Speaking of signs…there is a garage sale sign ahead. Turn left here."

So much for my serious talk about looking for God's sign. Or was it?

The man at the garage sale saw my lack of enthusiasm about his sale and sought to help me. "Hey, my neighbor just decided to have a sale. If you look, you can see the sign." I looked at him with a start. I thought, *Boy, wasn't that an appropriate choice of words for what I am stewing about.*

I walked across the yard and knocked on the open door to the neighbor's basement. "Hi," she greeted me. "I just put the sign up."

Ha! Those words again.

"Come on down," she invited. "I just started putting things out."

She pointed to her right, and I turned the corner at the bottom of the steps. There stood a six-foot table with a red tablecloth and Tiffany lamp on it. The lamp provided the only light in an otherwise darkened basement. There on the table, in an almost halo-like circle of light, sat a children's book on Jonah and the whale. I just stood there looking at it. Was this a sign or a strange coincidence?

I bought the book for a quarter. I walked back to the car and shared the event with my wife. We both laughed in disbelief and drove to the next garage sale. I must say I had my doubts about this "sign" and questioned God's involvement in what just happened.

We went to four more sales that morning, and all four prominently displayed the exact same version of Jonah and the whale. I bought them all. I finally acknowledged the message God was sending me. I still have all five copies of that book on Jonah, just to remind me of the work I need to do.

I guess I am in great company. God gave Moses a couple of signs at the burning bush (Exodus 4:2–9). Gideon asked God to give him a sign, so he would know he was acting on behalf of the Lord (Judges 6:1–39). Today I talk to church groups about the use of story-telling with children and adults.

So now it is your turn. Read this book several times. Learn the skills that will make you a more effective teacher and change the lives of your students.

*

The more words students hear and understand, the better chance they will recognize the same words in print.

Chapter Fifteen

*

ORGANIZING A STORYTELLING EVENT

Written by Karen Wollscheid and Nan Kammann-Judd

Karen Wollscheid is the business manager/event coordinator for Illinois Storytelling, Inc., producers of the Illinois Storytelling Festival and other events in northern Illinois. She is also business manager for Northlands Storytelling Network and artistic director of the Riverbend Storytelling Festival in West Bend, Wisconsin. She comes to the storytelling community with experience in marketing, advertising, graphic design, fund-raising, and board development. She is an active member of the National Storytelling Network's special interest group for event organizers, assisting with the mentorship program and producer's guide.

Nan Kammann-Judd, former director of the St. Louis Storytelling Festival, serves on their planning committee. Nan served six years on the National Storytelling Network's board of directors. She is on the board of directors of Illinois Storytelling, Inc., and the Honorary Chair of the 2003 National Conference on Storytelling in Chicago.

Now that you have discovered the wonderful world of storytelling, it's natural to want to share it with people in your community. Our ideas and suggestions are like a road map to help you do just that; we'll be your guide through the many little steps to get you where you want to go.

Perhaps you have the vision to start a storytelling ministry within your church. Here is a short list of ideas:

- Have an afternoon or evening of stories at the church.

- Start a storytelling group that performs in church services. This could be Bible stories, the history of hymns, special seasons of the year, or stories that illustrate the sermon.

- Take storytellers to those who are confined: homebound people, hospital patients, or prisoners.

- Provide a family storytelling concert at a church, city park, campground, RV park, local library, community center, etc.

- Start a storytelling club for senior citizens, where they can share memories with each other or bring in schoolchildren for a living history session.

- Conduct an outdoor storytelling festival under big-top tents. (This is the most ambitious.)

The following information will serve as a guide to your planning process. We've distilled the process of preparing a storytelling event into twelve steps (not to be confused with the fourteen steps to creating a story that John shared with you earlier in this manual).

1. IDENTIFY YOUR OBJECTIVE

Consider why you are creating this storytelling event or ministry. What do you hope to accomplish with it? Take your written answers and write an objective statement.

2. GATHER A PLANNING COMMITTEE

Next, build a base of supporters who will help nourish, guide, and enliven your progress. It can consist of businesspeople, fund-raisers, teachers, storytellers, church members, story listeners, and staff. A planning committee will help identify and recruit the support you need for the event and become a pool of ideas for the program.

Schedule regular meetings. This will make it easier to delegate and track responsibilities. The dynamics and talents of a group will exceed anything you have on your own.

The basic planning cycle for a large event is a year and a half. This may seem long, but you will need this time to allow for marketing and fund-raising.

3. PLAN THE SCOPE OF THE EVENT

It is best to hold a storytelling event in a quiet, contained, inviting space. Of course, there are festivals held on windswept moors overlooking the sea, but it is hard to compete with the sounds of wind and sea and beautiful terrain. On the other hand, a dreary, dark, stuffy room isn't inviting either.

Storytellers usually require little in the way of equipment. However, make sure the site has good lighting and a good sound system. Storytellers need to be seen and heard.

Keep in mind that, as with any event, it is better to fill a small space to capacity than to have a large space half full.

Here are some questions to ask as you consider locations.

- Will the event be for a church, a group of churches, a storytelling guild, or a community?
- Will it take place at one location or several?
- Do you want to hold your event indoors or outdoors?
- Is the space appropriate for a storytelling event? If not, what changes would be required?
- Will the space meet the needs of your audience?
- Will the space be provided free, or do you anticipate a fee?
- Will the space have staff and support services?
- Is there adequate parking?
- Is the location accessible for the disabled?

4. SELECT THE RIGHT STORYTELLERS

You may consider selecting storytellers to be the fun part, but don't let it fool you. Match the scope of the event with the abilities of the tellers.

When you talk to a prospective storyteller, examine your expectations. The key is to give the storytellers as much information about the event as you can, so they are able to give you the best possible performance. They will want to know facts about how often they will tell stories, how many days you'll expect them to perform, and what time slots they will fill.

FRIENDS— This is not the time to use a storyteller just because he/she is a friend. Ask the committee to establish this as a firm rule—like the law of the Medes and the Persians, which cannot be changed. We will only choose storytellers whose abilities match the scope of the event.

REPUTATION— Choosing the wrong storyteller for an occasion can decrease attendance for future events. We had one who told three stories about babies dying. It did not fit the occasion or our type of audience. Our attendance was down the following year. Carefully select your storytellers because your reputation is constantly being evaluated.

FEES— You may think storytellers are paid well for an hour or two on stage. Keep in mind that much of their work occurs before a performance. The fees for storytellers vary according to the region of the country and from one type of venue to another. Contact another event in your state that is similar to yours and ask what is the proper rate for storytellers.

BUDGET— If you have more than one storyteller, it is best to pay all of them the same fee. Pay mileage or airfare if they are traveling from a distance. Meals and housing should be provided for out-of-town performers.

QUESTIONS— When hiring storytellers, here is a list of questions to consider.

- What is the theme of your event?
- What do you expect from the storytellers?
- How many do you need?
- What kind of storytellers would be appropriate?
- What is your budget, and how many people can you afford to pay, house, feed, and transport?

- What mix of storytellers will make a complete and fulfilling program?
- Will they all be paid and treated the same?
- Will your expectations for local, regional, and national storytellers be different?
- What will be the selection process?

NUMBER OF STORYTELLERS— Your event will be fine if your budget allows for only one storyteller. If you are fortunate enough to be able to have several storytellers, make your selection as varied as possible. Look for people who can provide a little humor, some thoughtful whimsy, some stories of mystery, and so on. Occasionally you can get all this in one person. Other times, a group with diverse talents will provide the entire program for you.

INTERPRETATION FOR THE DEAF— Consider hiring sign language interpreters or asking a church to provide them for you. Most states have a registry of interpreters or referral services. Private referral services are also commonly listed in the Yellow Pages.

5. SET THE DATE

Try to select a date that has the fewest conflicts with other events in your community. Check with your Convention and Visitors Bureau or the Community Calendar of Events about scheduled events in your area.

6. DETERMINE HOW THE EVENT WILL BE FINANCED

Give careful thought and planning to determine the cost of your event. Deal with this early in the process to sustain an event after the first year.

- Sometimes a local church or group of churches will pay for a Christian storytelling event.
- You may want to charge a fee for admission, write for grants, or both.
- In some states there is funding for the arts from an arts council or regional arts commission.
- Perhaps an individual, corporation, or local foundation would be willing to underwrite all or part of the costs.
- Many sponsors do what is called "in-kind" participation (provide site facilities, staff, food, advertising, etc.). These are as valuable as monetary contributions.

- Some companies offer employees cash-match donations, or encourage employees to volunteer at community events.

Eventually you will be established, and people will see the benefit of the event. For now be brave; endure a little rejection; and ask for support, sponsorship, and contributions. This process will get easier as your event matures.

As much as possible, diversify your funding options. This will provide a safety net in case any one of the funding sources falls through.

Be realistic about having a staff person do this challenging work for you.

Think of fund-raising as friend-raising. Once a company or individual agrees to support your event, have a plan for recognizing and thanking them. Nurture and develop each relationship. They are friends who are helping you, and they need to be treated as such.

For example, our festival has been fortunate to have developed a lasting relationship with a professional photographer. He offered to take photos *pro bono* if we would pay for film and development. His family has enjoyed the festival, and we have given him full credit for his work. His photography has been helpful in promoting our marketing efforts. We are careful to keep him informed about our work and his contribution to the health of the organization.

7. LAY OUT THE OVERALL PLAN

A plan is a tool that tells you how you are going to accomplish the task. Make it easy, logical, and comprehensive. Think big, but plan small. This may seem the most tedious step. Still, it is essential.

Visualize what a successful event would look like, try to anticipate each aspect, and write it down. Once it is written, follow the plan to reach your goal.

After you've been through the complete cycle, the written plan gives you a tool to evaluate what you will do differently the next time. Think of the first plan as a rough draft. You won't have the final draft until the event is over.

The planning process would be to begin with a year-round calendar; select committee chairs and assign responsibilities; lay out timelines for meetings, confirmations, marketing, reservations, site selection, scheduling, storyteller selection; and create job descriptions.

When you have your basic structure and expectations in place, you should arrive with enough time, energy, and resources to respond effectively to any surprises. You will have at least a few surprises.

8. BUILD A PRODUCTION STAFF

The key to any successful event is finding and developing a successful staff. Delegating responsibilities will keep everyone sane during the planning and production process. Some committee areas of responsibility include:

- Site selection
- Storyteller selection
- Ticket sales
- Decorations
- Refreshments
- Setup—chairs, stage, sound, lighting, signs, etc.
- Cleanup
- Publicity (print materials, press releases, website, printed program)
- Storyteller hospitality (pick up at airport, travel between hotel and event site, food, needs at event site)
- On-site coordinator (familiar with sound systems, electrical hookups, locations of water fountains and restrooms)

Okay, we'll admit it. We're giving you a lot of lists. But a list makes it easier to hand the responsibility to someone else.

9. DEVELOP A MARKETING STRATEGY

Prepare a mailing list that is specific to the audience you want to reach. Direct mail is an expensive way to advertise, but specific mailing is effective. Also, develop an e-mail list.

Put posters and flyers in places that will attract your prospective audience.

Develop your own website or use your organization's existing one, and be sure to put your website's address on all printed materials.

Write press releases, and get them to the newspapers at least six weeks in advance. You can list the event with the local radio and television stations on their calendar of events. This is a free service to the community. Contact the Community Events editor of your local newspaper to arrange for a reporter and photographer to come to the event. Ask everyone on your committees to sell reduced-rate tickets in advance.

If you are going to provide deaf interpreters, place flyers at deaf clubs, schools, newsletters, and websites. Indicate that the event will be signed for the deaf in all your print media.

10. ALLOW FOR STORYTELLING DIFFERENCES

Here are a few special considerations for storytelling events.

The performance area should be clean, free of obstructions, and should never be in front of a bright window. It is hard for the audience to look into light or have outside distractions take attention away from the performance. It is best to have the storyteller's back to a wall or curtain, away from restrooms and exits.

Make sure storytellers and event producers talk to one another on a regular basis. Both will have input as to how the program could flow better. Discuss the stories that storytellers plan to tell and make sure they are appropriate for the group. Knowing these expectations will help a teller choose the best material. More than any other type of performer, storytellers can shape the programs to the individual situations. Also, know whether your storytellers will allow you to photograph or audiotape the event. Make these arrangements in advance of the performance date, and in writing.

Check with your storytellers on what they prefer in the way of a microphone: a stand, handheld, or clip-on. An excellent sound system is crucial. They will need a stool on stage with a small table nearby to hold a glass or bottle of water.

Children ages eight or younger usually prefer to sit on the floor near the stage. Most storytellers enjoy this, but only if parents are encouraged to sit on the floor with their children. It is hard for the audience to enjoy a performance if kids in front are unruly while the parents chat in the back of the room.

11. SCHEDULE A SPECIAL EVENT FOR VOLUNTEERS

Invite volunteers and workers to an informal get-together with the storytellers before everything gets started. After the event, plan a special time to congratulate each other on a job well done. This is a time to reflect on the blessings of the event, what was accomplished, who was there, and how people were impacted.

12. HAVE FUN!

If you have never planned a storytelling event, you are about to enter a whole new world of excitement and blessings. You will experience many rewards despite all the planning and potential headaches. You will enjoy seeing the happy faces and hearing the applause of an audience. You are about to meet and work with new friends; together you will have a great influence upon the community.

Remember: those who are experienced at putting on storytelling events are more than willing to share their expertise with you.

ADAPTING AN ADULT SHORT STORY

When a story is written for adults, the writer does not have the advantage of using facial expressions, body movements, dramatic pauses, changes in voice, and so forth. Therefore, it is filled with added descriptions that are meaningful to a reading audience.

All of this wonderful written description is cumbersome to a storyteller. Still, if it is a great story and you want to tell it, there are two ways to approach an adult-level written short story.

The first option is to remain close to the original interpretation of the author. This requires a monumental amount of work, and the storyteller usually is forced to memorize large portions of the story. I don't recommend this approach unless you have an extremely good reason to do so.

The second option is to adapt the story to your personality and situation. This is a more sensible route to take if you want to tell the written story. You use the plot, but you are *not* limited to the original interpretation.

Here are several tips that will help you make the story your own:

1. LEARN THE BASIC PLOT

Read the story several times. Once you feel you are familiar with the plot, put it away and don't look at it again, or at least not until you have developed your own version of it. If you look back at this point, it is because you want to "correct" how you are telling the story. Don't do it. You must separate how the author wrote the story from how you tell it.

2. REDUCE THE NUMBER OF MAIN CHARACTERS

Written stories have the luxury of using many prominent characters in the plot. Storytellers must limit themselves to three characters at the most. Two is even better. Which two or three people have to be in the story? Think of ways you can remove the others from the plot, or make them a minor element.

3. REDUCE THE STORY TO ITS SIMPLEST FORM

The objective of this tip is to eliminate the author's written descriptions. It is what I call "sterilizing the story." In reality, you are taking all of the life out of it, but don't worry; I will help you put your own life into it.

The best way to sterilize a story is to tell a quick version of it to someone. I usually do this when I am driving somewhere with my wife. I say, "Let me tell you about an interesting story I read." I then tell her the essence of it in about two minutes. This brings the story down to its simplest form. It is now prepared for reconstruction.

Once you have taken these three steps, you are ready to take the story through the fourteen steps in preparing a story for telling. Remember: don't look back at the original story. Each time you revisit it, you are undoing what you have accomplished.

—— *time to practice* ——

Here are two ideas to try:

✻ Choose a short story from O. Henry, and take it through the three steps provided in this appendix.

✻ Choose a chapter from a well-known book such as:

• *The Adventures of Huckleberry Finn,* by Mark Twain

• *Little Women,* by Louisa May Alcott

• *Left Behind* series, by Tim LaHaye and Jerry B. Jenkins

• A biography of a famous Christian

Take the chapter through the three steps in this appendix; then prepare it into a story you can tell.

FIVE STARTER STORIES

THE LONELY SHEPHERD BOY

A young shepherd boy was tending his sheep out on the meadow. It was a lonely job, so he thought of a way he could have some fun. He rushed toward the village crying out, "Wolf! Wolf!" Several men from the village grabbed their guns and ran to help him. They stayed with him for a while, but when no wolf appeared, the men returned to the village.

A few days later, the shepherd boy was again feeling lonely, so he tried the same trick, and again the villagers ran to help him. When no wolf appeared this time, the men knew they had been fooled, and they were not happy about it.

The next week, a wolf really did come out from the forest and began circling the flock of sheep. The boy cried much louder than before, "Wolf! Wolf!" But this time, nobody came to help him. That day the wolf killed several sheep from the boy's flock.

When the boy complained to the villagers, one of the wise old men told him,

✳

"A liar will not be believed, even when he speaks the truth."

✳

THE DONKEY'S IMPRESSIVE ATTIRE

A small donkey was tired of his humble estate, always serving others. He wondered what it would feel like to be "king of the beasts." One day he was strolling through the woods when he came upon a large lion's skin that hunters had laid out to dry.

He looked at it for a while and got an idea. He worked his way into the lion's skin, which actually covered him quite well. Then he strutted through the forest, back toward his village.

As he moved along the path, the other beasts saw him and made way for him. They had respect for this animal with the elegant coat.

As the little donkey neared his village, he spied his master, who didn't seem to recognize him. The donkey was so proud of himself, he couldn't contain his joy any longer. He burst out with a loud "Hee Haw." Immediately his master came toward him. He pulled off the lion's skin, put a rope around the donkey's neck, and led him back to the barn, where he waited for his next assignment of chores. The donkey stood there with his head down and finally said to himself,

*

There is value in keeping your mouth shut.

*

A GIRL AND HER DREAMS

Miriam was the only daughter of a farmer who earned his living by selling the milk from his cows. She was an attractive girl, but her family was so poor she had no money for pretty clothes or fancy hairdos. The young men of her town did not recognize her beauty and turned up their noses at her.

One day her father said to her, "Today you may sell a bucket of milk and buy eggs so you can hatch some chickens of your own. Then you can sell their eggs and buy beautiful clothes."

Miriam began to dream about her chickens. In her head she was counting the eggs she would sell each day, and the money she would have for new clothes.

Before she started to the market that day, she carefully put the bucket of milk on top of her head. As she walked along, she imagined herself wearing her new clothes and all the young men trying to get her attention. She would not even look at them, but would simply turn up her nose at them and…As she put her nose into the air, her pail of milk tipped and spilled down all over the dry ground beneath her feet. She watched the milk soak into the ground, along with all of her dreams.

*

Don't count your chickens before they hatch.

*

THE FATHER, SON, AND DONKEY

A farmer and his son were taking their donkey into town to sell him. As they strolled along, they passed a neighbor lady. "What a waste," she said. "One of you ought to ride on the donkey." The farmer stopped and placed his son on the donkey's back.

Next they walked past an old man working in his garden. "How shameful," he remarked. "Does your boy have no respect for his elders?" Immediately the boy got off the donkey and his father got on.

They passed a group of children playing who taunted the boy, "Is your father always so inconsiderate? Why does he make you walk while he rides?" At that remark, the father reached down and lifted up the boy, setting him in front of him.

The donkey walked much slower now, bearing his heavy load. At the edge of town, they passed the blacksmith. He paused from his work, looked up, and scolded, "How cruel of you to overwork your donkey this way. The two of you are strong enough to carry him."

Awkward as it was, the father and his son managed to pick up the donkey and carry him through the town. When they came to the man who was to buy the donkey, he replied, "I certainly wouldn't want to buy a donkey that can't even walk to market."

*

You can't please all the people all the time.

*

BIG FRIEND, LITTLE FRIEND

A big lion was napping one warm afternoon when suddenly a small creature ran over the top of his nose and awakened him. With one swipe of his paw, he caught the little gray mouse.

The lion roared, "How could you be so foolish as to walk across my nose? I think I will eat you."

"Oh, no!" cried the mouse. "Please have mercy on me. I will never let it happen again. If you will let me go, someday I will find a way to do a favor for you." The whole idea of the mouse doing him a favor made the lion laugh. He admired the courage of the little mouse and finally decided to let her go.

Some time later, a group of clever hunters caught the lion in a huge net. They hung the net in a sturdy tree and went away to get a cage in which to put the lion.

As the great lion groaned in fear, the little mouse recognized the voice of her friend who had shown her kindness. She saw the lion's desperate situation and cried out, "I will help you." She climbed onto the net and began nibbling as fast as she could. She chewed right through the ropes of the net, and it came unraveled, allowing the lion to escape. The lion learned that…

✳

Sometimes your littlest friends are your greatest friends.

✳

STORYTELLING RESOURCES

STORYTELLING AND THE FAMILY

The Storyteller's Start-Up Book, by Margaret Read MacDonald, August House, 1993;
ISBN 0-87483-305-1

Telling Your Own Stories, by Donald Davis, August House, 1993;
ISBN 0-87483-235-7

The Parent's Guide to Storytelling, by Margaret Read MacDonald, August House, 1995;
ISBN 0-87483-618-2

Ready-to-tell Tales and *More Ready-to-tell Tales from Around the World,* edited by David Holt and
Bill Mooney, August House, 1994 and 2000; ISBN 0-87483-381-7 and ISBN 0-87483-583-6

Best Loved Folktales of the World, edited by Joanna Cole, Doubleday, 1982;
ISBN 0-38518-949-4. This one is out of print, so look for it in the library.

Favorite Folktales from around the World, edited by Jane Yolen, Random House, 1988;
ISBN 0-394-75188-4

The Paper Bag Princess (and many other titles) by Robert Munsch, Annick, 1993; ISBN 0-92023-616-2

The board game *Lifestories* by Family Narratives, Inc.

STORYTELLING AND THE CHURCH

Ambassadors for Christ, edited by John Woodbridge, Chicago: Moody, 1994.

> This collection is a treasury of stories about great leaders in the modern-day Christian church.

Great Leaders of the Christian Church, edited by John Woodbridge, Chicago: Moody, 1988.

> This reference tool contains articles about sixty-four of the most influential people in church history.

A Treasury of Jewish Folklore, by Nathan Ausubel, New York: Crown, 1975.

> This collection is a treasury of parables, legends, wisdom, and folktales from the Jewish tradition.

The Book of Virtues: A Treasury of Great Moral Stories, edited by William J. Bennett, editor, New York: Simon & Schuster, 1993.

> A helpful resource if you're looking for a story to illustrate a certain character trait, such as courage or honesty. It includes a wide range of stories.

Tales of the Frontier: From Lewis and Clark to the Last Roundup, by Everett Dick, Univ. of Nebraska Press, 1963.

> A wonderful collection of American frontier tales.

Cajun Folktales, by J. J. Reneaux, Little Rock: August House, 1992.

> This collection includes a variety of tales, from humorous to scary. It also has a number of delightful animal fables.

The Story of the Church, by Robert G. Clouse, Richard V. Pierard, Edwin M. Yamauchi, Chicago: Moody, 2003.

BIBLICAL RESOURCES FOR STORYTELLING

The New Manners and Customs of Bible Times, by Ralph Gower, Chicago: Moody, 1987.

> A thorough and fascinating study of biblical culture, designed to improve your understanding of God's Word. Contains color photography, diagrams, maps, and charts.

Story Journey: An Invitation to the Gospel as Storytelling, by Thomas Boomershine, Nashville: Abingdon, 1988.

> Boomershine gives an inspiring, instructive introduction to the purpose and methods of biblical storytelling. Using passages from the Gospels as illustrations, he shows the basic approach to analyzing and interpreting a text for oral delivery.

The Sower's Seeds, by Brian Cavanaugh, New York: Paulist, 1990.

> In addition to this first book, Cavanaugh has published a number of other books in this series. This collection of folktales, parables, and anecdotes from around the world provides a treasure trove of stories to use in storytelling ministries. Each book contains a helpful index which arranges the stories according to themes.

Commentary on the Whole Bible, by Matthew Henry, Grand Rapids: Zondervan, 1961.

> This is a classic Bible resource, and it provides excellent insights into biblical passages.

The Interpreter's Bible, New York: Abingdon-Cokesbury, 1952.

> This series contains volumes on all the books of the Old and New Testaments, providing a wealth of footnotes. This is an excellent source for understanding the various nuances and meanings of the text and for tracing word use.

The Interpreter's Dictionary of the Bible, four volumes. New York: Abingdon, 1962.

> This is an excellent resource for researching the historical context of a Bible passage and for gathering information about the daily life of the period.

The Communicator's Commentary, by Lloyd J. Ogilvie, general editor, Waco, Texas: World Books.

> This series was written for people who want to communicate the riches of the Scriptures. It offers insights and details not found in other commentaries. Each volume focuses on a specific book of the Bible, and the editors are experts in their areas.

The World Jesus Knew, by Anne Punton, Chicago: Moody 2003.

The Application Commentary: From Biblical Text to Contemporary Life, by Terry Muck, general editor, Grand Rapids: Zondervan.

> This unique commentary set places the text in historical context and offers a contemporary application.

The Storyteller's Companion to the Bible, by Michael E. Williams, Nashville: Abingdon.

> This ongoing series of books published on books in the Old and New Testaments. It includes stories by well-known storytellers and helpful tips about reinterpreting a Bible story.

Stories for Telling: A Treasury for Christian Storytellers, by William R. White, Minneapolis: Augsburg, 1992.

> This book provides theory and practical examples of biblical storytelling. Written by a storytelling minister, these books contain numerous sample stories.

STORYTELLING AND EDUCATION

Tales from the Hills, by Dr. Michael Lockett, is an audio production featuring the author telling eight time-tested stories for children and their families. You will find this audio production, as well as others, on our website—*www.christianstorytelling.com.*

eTips@storydynamics.com, by Doug Lipman, offers an online monthly newsletter of storytelling tips, ideas, resources, and events.

ORGANIZING A STORYTELLING EVENT

The Organizer's Special Interest Group (SIG) of the National Storytelling Network has a number of services available to help new storytelling organizers throughout the country. Go to their website: www.storynet.org/nsn/sig.htm for information on the SIG, its mentorship program, and its producer's guide; call (317) 576-9848 for more information.

The National Storytelling Network maintains a list of storytellers and storytelling events around the country. Their website is www.storynet.org; or call 1-800-525-4514 for more information.

SINCE 1894, Moody Publishers has been dedicated to equip and motivate people to advance the cause of Christ by publishing evangelical Christian literature and other media for all ages, around the world. As a ministry of the Moody Bible Institute of Chicago, proceeds from the sale of this book help to train the next generation of Christian leaders.

If we may serve you in any way in your spiritual journey toward understanding Christ and the Christian life, please contact us at www.moodypublishers.com.

"All Scripture is God-breathed and is useful for teaching, rebuking, correcting and training in righteousness, so that the man of God may be thoroughly equipped for every good work."

—*2 TIMOTHY 3:16, 17*

MOODY
PUBLISHERS
THE NAME YOU CAN TRUST®